SNAKE BITE

The smaller the child, the more severe the problem. Also, bites on the chest, head and neck are more dangerous than ones on the extremities. The more rapidly the bitten area becomes swollen and red, the more venom has been injected. However, assume that all bites are serious. If your child is bitten:

POISONING

Any nonfood substance swallc potential poison.

1. Get the container and then poison-control center or local eme be asked the exact brand name a

2. Do not make the child vomit unless you are told to do so. Some substances do more harm coming up than staying in the stomach.

3. If you are instructed

emergency room, take the container with you.

4. Drive slowly and carefully. You have time—you don't need to run red lights.

BEE, WASP AND ANT STINGS

See other side for serious allergic reactions. For routine bites and stings:

1. Remove the stinger with a scraping motion, using your fingernail or a clean, dull knife. Do *not* pull out.

2. Apply cold compresses to relieve pain, but do *not* use ice.

3. If you suspect a black-widow-spider bite, watch for abdominal pain, muscle spasms, vomiting, sweating, swollen eyes, and severe pain. In a baby, the only sign may be uncontrollable crying. If this happens, take your child to an emergency room.

---

2. If you can, either identify the snake or kill it and take it with you to an emergency facility.

3. If the bite is on an arm or leg, keep the bitten area below the level of the heart.

4. Get the child to medical care immediately. If more than an hour away, check by phone with a medical facility.

5. Do not give any medicines, especially aspirin.

6. Do not cut the bite or attempt to suck the venom out with your mouth.

BLEEDING

1. Apply constant pressure with gauze pads or a clean cloth directly over the cut for several minutes.

2. If possible, elevate the cut above the level of the heart, unless you suspect a fracture.

3. If bleeding soaks through the bandages, add more on top. Don't remove the bottom ones.

4. Seek medical assistance for severe bleeding only after you've tried to stop the bleeding, unless someone else is available to call for help sooner.

NOSEBLEEDS

1. Sit the child up, head slightly forward.

2. Pinch the nostrils between your thumb and first finger for 5 to 10 minutes. Don't cheat and peek every few seconds to see if bleeding has stopped.

3. If you can't stop the nosebleed, call your

SPLINTERS

1. Clean the area with soap and water. If the splinter is wood, clean but don't soak.

2. Gently remove with clean tweezers or a needle washed with alcohol or heated with a match.

3. Wash the area again after the splinter is out.

4. If the splinter won't come out, see your pediatrician within 24 hours to avoid infection.

BROKEN BONES

1. If there's any possibility of the neck or spine being injured, or if a leg shows an obvious deformity, do not move or pick up the child. Call 911 for assistance.

MINOR BURNS

1. Immerse the burned area in cool

WHEN DO I CALL THE DOCTOR?

DOUBLEDAY

·

NEW YORK

·

LONDON

·

TORONTO

·

SYDNEY

·

AUCKLAND

When Do I Call the Doctor?

In just 60 seconds you can find the answers to more than 200 common, and not-so-common, childhood complaints from headache to hiccups, swimmer's ear to swollen glands, bedwetting to bumps and blisters, and many, many more.

LORAINE M. STERN, M.D.

PUBLISHED BY DOUBLEDAY
a division of Bantam Doubleday Dell Publishing Group, Inc.
666 Fifth Avenue, New York, New York 10103

DOUBLEDAY and the portrayal of an anchor with a dolphin
are registered trademarks of Doubleday,
a division of Bantam Doubleday Dell Publishing Group, Inc.

Designed by Liney Li

Library of Congress Cataloging-in-Publication Data

Stern, Loraine.
When do I call the doctor? / Loraine M. Stern.
p.   cm.
"In just 60 seconds you can find the answers to more than 200 . . .
childhood complaints . . ."
Includes index.
1. Pediatrics—Popular works.   I. Title.
RJ61.S8933   1993
618.92—dc20   92-7436
                                CIP

ISBN 0-385-41991-0

This, and everything else, for Jack.

⊡ ACKNOWLEDGMENTS ⊡

My partners, Drs. Albert Melaragno and Kathy Brockett, deserve special thanks for reviewing material and indulging my need to write.

Thank you for advice, review, and encouragement: Esther Brudo, Ph.D.; John D'Ambola, M.D.; David Fleischer, M.D.; Arthur Garfinkel, M.D.; Bernard Raskin, M.D.; Arthur Vatz, M.D.; and Lucille Moss, Medical Librarian.

Thank you to my patients, who make me laugh and cry and provided rich material for this book, and to my office staff, who make trying to work and write at the same time easy and fun.

My agent, Wendy Weil, and my editor, John Duff, helped me realize my goal, and my husband, Jack Nides, makes my life and work possible and joyous.

CONTENTS

II. HEAD, EYES, EARS, NOSE, & THROAT 49

CONTENTS · xi

WHEN DO I CALL THE DOCTOR?

The days of the extended family are gone—at least in North America. No longer is there likely to be an aunt or cousin or grandmother at hand to reassure you that what's happening to your child is normal or to advise you about the problems that she successfully handled herself. Grandmothers these days are not at home baking cookies and helping to raise children like Aunt Bea in Mayberry. They are often either too far away to help with day-to-day issues or are still involved in their own careers. Pediatricians have now taken on much of the role that the extended family used to assume.

The purpose of this book is threefold—to save you worry, to make sure your child is seen early for a serious problem, and sometimes to save you an unnecessary visit to the doctor's office or the emergency room.

Every child is different, every set of parents is different. This book is not meant to replace your own pediatrician because I cannot know you, your anxiety threshold, or your child. The most important ingredient is what you bring to this text—your own judgment and needs. If you feel there is something wrong, call or see your pediatrician even if your child fits every criterion for normalcy and there is nothing you can put your finger on. The next section, "How to Know if Your Child Is Seriously Ill," emphasizes that there are intangible factors that can make a parent worry. These vague feelings may be nothing but sometimes can be caused by subtle signs of a serious problem.

What I have found in browsing through most child health care books is that too often you have to be able to name the problem before you can look up the remedy. In this book, I have tried to make it possible for you to look up your child's symptoms or rash, figure out what it could be, and find out what your best course of action should be: to do nothing, to call or see your pediatrician soon, or to go to an emergency room right away. Once the diagnosis is clear, your pediatrician and a good child care book can give you more detailed information on how to treat it and what to expect.

Although this is not a how-to-book, I sometimes found it irresistible to give you a few hints to help make your child more comfortable until you can see your pediatrician.

This book deals only with children from birth to the beginnings of adolescence. Once a child reaches the teens, everything changes and becomes more complicated.

I chose the specific signs and symptoms I deal with most often over the telephone with my patients. I left out situations in which you already know you should call your doctor—if you see lice on your child's hair, for example, I have no doubt you will be on the phone immediately.

Being a parent, especially a first-time parent, is never easy, but I hope this book offers some reassurance and some useful information.

HOW TO KNOW
IF YOUR CHILD IS
SERIOUSLY ILL

It is normal and understandable to be frightened when your child is sick, especially if this is your first child and you have had no experience with sick children. Even pediatricians who can confidently distinguish critically ill from less seriously ill patients become a little crazy when their own children are sick.

One of the reasons we need to be more careful with children is that they have a tendency to go from being a little sick to critically ill all of a sudden. Adults have more reserves. An adult who is becoming dehydrated, for example, may take hours to days to become seriously depleted, whereas an infant may look just a little sick for several hours and then suddenly collapse.

The best way to be prepared for extreme emergency is to take a CPR class from your local Red Cross, hospital, or civic organization and repeat the class every year or two to keep fresh. Most of the time, however, you will need to make more subtle judgments about just how sick your child is.

Many of the signs in the following list are vague— how do you measure irritability, for example? Nevertheless, you are a good judge of your child's normal behavior and just how far from the norm he or she is behaving at the moment. An investigative reporter told me that one of the clues that leads her to a story is JDLR—"Just Doesn't Look Right." The same is true about your child. If there is nothing you can put your finger on but your child just doesn't look right, get to the office or emergency room promptly. The earlier treatment is begun, the better the chance for full recovery.

WHEN TO WORRY

Infants

Inability to suck for two or more feedings, or a poor suck which tires right away.

Weak, mousy cry rather than the usual strong, lusty one.

Irritability—not seeming comfortable no matter what you do, and crying inconsolably.

Acting as though movement is painful.

Crying without tears, not urinating for more than 6 to 8 hours, sunken eyes.

Any fever over 100.4° Fahrenheit in a baby under 2 months.

All ages

Cool, clammy skin with paleness, gray or dusky blue color (when you press on the skin with a finger, it takes more than a second or so for color to return).

Limpness, lack of strength or decreased movement to the limbs or head.

A vacant expression in eyes that are usually alert and lively.

Poor coordination, staggering, confusion.

Rapid, shallow breathing. Do not confuse this with

the rapid breathing that accompanies a high fever; if your child appears otherwise well, bring the temperature down before worrying about this. See pages 231–34 about treating fever.

Noisy breathing with grunting, crowing, or other abnormal sounds.

Sinking in of the area above or below the rib cage or the spaces between the ribs with each breath.

A moan, groan, grunt, or "uh" sound with each breath.

A stiff neck accompanied by fever, irritability, or any of the other signs of illness.

Sunken eyeballs, dry mouth, loss of skin elasticity.

Lack of eye contact. This is the most telling sign for pediatricians; even children who feel terrible with a minor illness can still look people in the eye and object to their presence; a child with a serious illness often stares into space, seemingly oblivious of surroundings.

HOW TO MAKE
THE BEST USE OF
THE TELEPHONE

· WHAT TO CALL ABOUT ·

Telephoning for advice is most useful for simple, short-term problems—what to do about a sore throat or vomiting, how much to worry about a fever or cough, should you bring your child in right now or can you wait a little longer? Complex issues such as behavior, sleep, or school problems are better dealt with face to face at an appointment with your pediatrician.

· WHEN TO CALL ·

You should feel free to call your pediatrician any time, but if you are not dealing with an emergency, there are some times that are better than others.

Just as in an auto repair shop, Monday mornings tend to be busier than the rest of the week. Calling your pediatrician's office at that time may be frustrating because of the volume of patients in the office and backed-up phone calls. Wait until later in the day on Mondays if you can.

Pediatricians are accustomed to middle-of-the-night calls, and if you are frightened in the wee hours of the morning, do not hesitate to call. Also, children have an uncanny ability to keep their temperature down until five o'clock on Friday evening, when it shoots up to 104°F.

If a problem has been developing over several days, however—constipation, for example—most pediatricians would prefer that you wait until daylight hours.

Some pediatricians have "phone hours," usually an hour in the morning before the office opens and again in the late afternoon. During that time, the doctor personally answers calls about nonemergency problems. If you call after hours, the answering service will usually connect you with the doctor or nurse practitioner on call.

During office hours, however, the bulk of calls are taken by nurses or medical assistants who are trained to evaluate basic problems over the phone and refer more complex matters to the doctor. In my office, for example, the receptionists know that any infant under two months who has a fever must come in. I trust my nurses and medical assistants to decide, for example, when your one-year-old with vomiting and diarrhea can be treated at home for another few hours or if you need to come in right away.

If you want to talk directly to the doctor, ask, although usually you will have to wait a bit longer for a break between patients.

Ask the receptionist when you can expect to be called back if someone cannot take your call right away, and if you are not called back by then, put in another call. Even in the most efficient office or answering service, messages can be misplaced.

· PREPARING TO CALL ·

In recent years I take more and more after-hours calls about sick children from fathers rather than mothers. I am delighted by the new responsibilities fathers are assuming, but often, because he has not been caring for the child all day, the conversation goes something like this:

FATHER: Doctor Stern, Jason has a high fever.

ME: How high is it?

FATHER, turning from the phone: Honey, how high is it? (*Pause.*) A hundred and three under the arm.

ME: How long has he had it?

FATHER: Honey, how long has he had it? (*Pause.*) About two hours.

ME: How does he look to you?

FATHER: Wait a minute, he's in the other room.

It is your pediatrician's job, not yours, to extract and sort out information when you are worried about your child. Nevertheless, you will feel more in control and be able to communicate more effectively if you prepare a little before you call.

1. Take your child's temperature, if appropriate.

Report your child's temperature and the way that you took it—with a mercury thermometer, a digital electronic one, or a fever strip; under the arm, rectally, or orally. Do not correct up or down for what you may have been told should be a correction factor.

If your child has a high fever and is acting uncomfortable, treat the fever (see the chapter on fever), wait forty-five minutes to an hour and take another temperature before you call. Telling your pediatrician how your child looks and acts after the fever is down is important information.

2. Know your child's approximate weight.

Children's medicines are prescribed by weight as well as age. Although pediatricians know average weights for children at various ages, your child may be larger or smaller than average. You need not know to the nearest ounce, but look up how much your child weighed at the last office visit or the last baby book entry or put your child on the bathroom scale so that you can give your doctor a ball park idea.

3. Recall the names and dosages of any medication your child is taking and any that have caused reactions in the past.

Consider anything that is not food to be a medication, even vitamins, food supplements, eye drops, lotions, and ointments. All medications can have side effects, and some react adversely with each other. Children are particularly prone to absorb chemicals through their delicate skin. For example, calamine lotion mixed with Benadryl (Caladryl) dabbed onto chicken pox while you are also giving Benadryl by mouth can lead to an overdose.

In one recent case, I began to order some expensive tests to try to figure out a patient's strange symptoms when her mother remembered that she was applying an antibiotic solution to her child's face prescribed by a dermatologist. The child's symptoms turned out to be side effects of the medication.

Over the phone and without your child's chart at hand, your own doctor or the one taking the calls that night may not remember that your child has been taking an antiseizure medicine for the past year, that your child is on stimulant medication for school problems, or that your child is allergic to penicillin.

4. Tell your doctor if you have been giving leftover medication.

In the middle of the night it is hard to resist the temptation to give a little bit of penicillin that was left over after the last throat infection. You know you probably shouldn't, so you might want to avoid telling your doctor to avoid being yelled at.

The reason to tell your pediatrician is not just because confession is good for the soul but to save your child and your pocketbook from unnecessary procedures. If you have already given a day or two of penicillin, for example, a routine throat culture will be of little or no value, and other tests would be more revealing.

5. Remind the doctor of any chronic medical problems.

No matter how well your pediatrician knows your child, there are times, especially when awakened in the middle of the night, when we are not functioning on all cylinders.

The mother of a child who was new to my practice called late one night because her child had an eye infection. It sounded minor, so I told her to apply warm compresses and I would see him the next day. When he came in, I realized to my horror that this was a child with only one functioning eye, and it was that eye that was infected.

He was fine in a day or two, but I certainly would have responded differently had I realized what the situation was.

6. Have the name and number of your pharmacy handy.

Your doctor may want to call in a prescription to tide you over until you can bring your child to the office. Make sure the pharmacy is open.

7. Keep a pencil and paper at hand.

There are two reasons for this: first, so that you can write down all the questions you need answered before you call. Sometimes after I've talked at length with patients, they call back in five minutes because they have another question they forgot to ask.

More importantly, however, when you are worried and upset you may not be able to remember the details of your doctor's instructions without writing them down: were you supposed to give one ounce of clear liquid every two hours or two ounces every one hour?

8. Have your child nearby.

During your conversation with the doctor, questions may arise that you did not anticipate. When parents call about rashes, for instance, I often ask if the redness blanches when you press on it, and usually they have not checked for this. It is much easier if your child is near you rather than upstairs.

9. Before you hang up, ask how long you can expect this problem to last and what signs to worry about.

Knowing the duration and possible complications of any condition can save you considerable anxiety.

During flu season, for example, I always kick myself if I forget to tell patients that symptoms may last a few days. There's no point in calling the second day a child is sick with the flu because I wouldn't have expected any improvement.

WHAT SUPPLIES TO KEEP ON HAND

· MEDICATIONS ·

Children are unusually sensitive to the sound of pharmacists locking up for the night. As soon as business hours are over, I start receiving phone calls about earaches, fevers, cough—all of which can be at least temporarily relieved with medication so that parents and children can get some rest before being seen in the morning.

You do not need to have a whole pharmacy on hand. You will, however, be better able to help your child through the night if you have a basic store of medication. The most important medicines to keep on hand are:

1. Fever reducer/pain reliever

Acetaminophen (Tylenol, Tempra, Panadol, etc.) is available as drops, liquid, chewable tablets, pills, and suppositories. This safe and effective drug can relieve pain and reduce fever, and has very few side effects when given as directed.

You should have on hand not only the form that is appropriate for your child's age but also some suppositories in case your child is vomiting and cannot keep medicine down.

2. Antihistamine

Itching from chicken pox, insect bites, hives, and other rashes can make children miserable. Sneezing, itchy eyes, and a runny nose from exposure to an animal or something else to which your child is allergic can also cause misery. An antihistamine (Benadryl, for example) is effective not only in reducing discomfort but sometimes, in the case of an allergic reaction, even in curing the problem.

Be aware that there is a problem with antihistamines that is unique to children. While antihistamines make many adults and children sleepy, some children become stimulated and irritable. Instead of promoting sleep, therefore, they may prevent it. Unfortunately, there is no way to know how your child will react until you give a dose.

3. Cough medicine

Some antihistamines can also function as cough suppressants because of their sedative action, but it is more reliable to have a real cough suppressant on hand. Any over-the-counter cough medicine with dextromethorphan—usually one with DM in the name such as Robitussin DM—will do.

4. Ear drops for pain

Ear infections hurt more at night because lying down increases the pressure in the middle ear. Auralgan, Aurodex, or any other brand of anesthetic ear drops may get you through a painful night. *These are available only by prescription* and most families do not have them in their medicine cabinets unless their child has had an ear infection before. If your child is prone to ear infections, be sure to keep a bottle on hand.

The drops work a little better if you warm them

gently in a cup of hot water. Do not heat them in the microwave or you risk burning your child's ear.

5. Nose drops

Do not use decongestant nose drops such as Neosynephrine or Afrin routinely or your child may become dependent on them. Nevertheless, I have found that in the middle of the night there is nothing quite so effective with so few side effects to allow infants to drink their bottles and children to sleep.

Be sure you use a strength appropriate for your child's age and never use the drops more than two or three nights in a row.

Decongestant nose drops can also be helpful to control a nosebleed. Check with your pediatrician, however, before you use them.

Saltwater nose drops for infants are only an aid to removing mucus. They will not decongest the nose.

6. Syrup of ipecac

If you have a child under four in your house, the risk of accidental poisoning is always there. No matter how conscientious *you* are about locking up poisons, someone may come to visit with medication in a purse, a workman may leave something lying around, or suspicious mushrooms might pop up in your yard after a rain.

Syrup of ipecac is a reliable way to induce vomiting when your child has eaten or drunk something harmful. It is available without a prescription, but usually there will be no specific directions on the label except to "use as directed by a physician."

Never use ipecac without consulting your pediatrician first; not only does the dose vary with age and weight, but there are some poisons that should not be brought up. Having ipecac on hand is like having a fire extinguisher; you hope you never need it but it is there if you do.

· SUPPLIES ·

1. Thermometer

A mercury thermometer is the most accurate and reliable, but digital thermometers are fast and easy to read. The batteries may poop out at 3 A.M., however, so keep a mercury thermometer on hand even if you have a digital one.

2. Ice bag and hot water bottle

Although you can always wrap a plastic bag of ice cubes in a towel, an ice bag does not leak and is less likely to cause frostbite when applied to children's delicate skin.

A hot water bottle is safer than a heating pad for children, because it is almost impossible to be burned by a hot water bottle, which gradually cools as it sits. The steady heat of a heating pad can burn after a while.

3. Vaporizer or humidifier

Indoor air tends to be dry, especially if you live in a dry climate or when the heat is on in the winter. Colds and coughs can sometimes be relieved a little by humidifying the air in your child's bedroom during naps and nighttime sleep.

If you have a toddler in the house, it is probably safer to use a cool mist system. Children have been burned by falling onto hot steam units, or by pulling them over on themselves. Whether you use a hot steam or cool mist system, choose a model which includes a filter to remove impurities from the water.

· HELPING THE SITTER ·

If you use babysitters, be sure that they are confident about what to do if your child is sick or injured. Do not be afraid to pose "what if" questions before you trust them with your child. Make sure they are familiar with the location of all fire extinguishers and with the escape routes in case of fire.

It will help at moments of emergency if you have these additional things prepared:

1. Consent for treatment

For emergencies that threaten life or limb, any emergency facility will take necessary action. For anything less than that, however, they will need your consent. If you are not reachable and your child has a minor cut that needs stitches, the sitter and your child may wait for hours until your consent can be obtained.

It is a good idea to give your sitter a dated, signed note that says,

"I, _____ , parent of _____ allow (the sitter) to obtain any necessary emergency medical care for my child."

2. An emergency list next to the phone

Be sure to have an easily spotted list containing:

a. your pediatrician's number.

b. the number where you and your spouse can be reached.

c. the address and telephone number of your own house.

d. the name and phone number of a nearby neighbor and of a relative.

e. the telephone number of the emergency squad in your area—usually 911.

CHAPTER 1.

The
Newborn

Newborn babies up to two months are different from older infants. First of all, they do peculiar things. They snort, twitch, develop spots that come and go, spit up milk and sometimes even blood, and generally find ways to make parents, particularly first-time parents, crazy. They are also medically different from older babies. A six-month-old with a fever is most likely not seriously ill; a newborn with a fever must be treated as though there is a serious problem until proven otherwise.

Therefore, although the rest of this book is organized according to the area of your child's body that you might be concerned about, this chapter deals exclusively with all parts of the newborn. To find information about a specific issue, refer to Illustration 1.

1 | SOFT SPOT

The skull of an infant is not a solid mass of hardened bone like that of an adult. Instead, it is made up of several individual bones loosely joined together. Where four of these bones meet on top of the head, a diamond-shaped space is left open. It may be as small as a fingertip or up to an inch or more across. During the first eighteen

Problems in the newborn.
Locate the area you are
concerned about and find the
answer on the page listed.

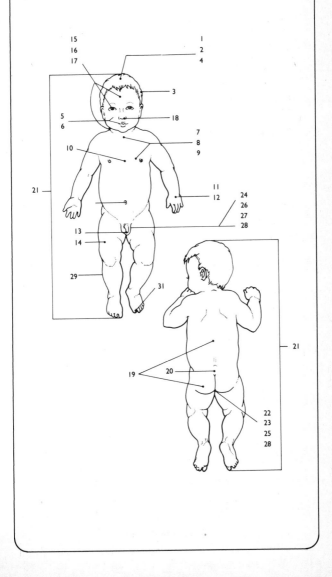

months to two years, this soft spot gradually disappears.

You may also find a small triangular soft spot in the back of the head, but that is usually gone by birth or disappears shortly afterward.

Some babies have no discernible soft spot at birth or it disappears abnormally early. As long as your pediatrician is pleased with how fast your baby's head is growing, there is no need to worry.

Even though there is no bone over the soft spot, tough membranes and fluid-filled space under the scalp protect the brain. You will not harm your baby by pressing down when shampooing or brushing hair. Don't be afraid of it.

When your baby is crying, the soft spot may protrude, but it should become flat or slightly sunken after the baby calms down. Also, when your baby is quiet, you may see regular pulsations. These are normal and are a reflection of your baby's heartbeat.

Persistent bulging of the soft spot, on the other hand, may signal a problem with excess pressure in your baby's brain.

♥ IT IS NORMAL FOR

· the soft spot to bulge intermittently and pulsate.

☎ CALL YOUR PEDIATRICIAN *IMMEDIATELY* IF

· the soft spot bulges and your baby is irritable, has a fever, is vomiting, or has any other signs of illness.

| 2 | RIDGES ON THE HEAD |

On the way through the birth canal during labor, your baby's head takes quite a beating. Because the bones of the skull are loosely connected, the pressure of labor can cause one or more of these bones to overlap another, creating a ridge that you can feel easily. If your baby has little or no hair, you may even see it. Usually the bones even out within a few weeks.

♥ IT IS NORMAL FOR

- a ridge or two to be seen or felt for several weeks after birth.

⊖ BRING IT TO YOUR PEDIATRICIAN'S ATTENTION AT THE NEXT CHECKUP IF

- the ridge persists after the second month and your child's head appears to be growing off kilter. This could be a sign of *craniosynostosis,* in which one or two bones stop growing prematurely. Because the skull can become distorted, surgery before age six months minimizes the chances of deformity and prevents possible pressure on the brain.

3	BUMP ON THE SIDE OF THE HEAD
	(CEPHALOHEMATOMA)

Another result of the banging around your baby's head endures during birth is a soft bump on one or both sides of the head. It may be small or up to several inches across and feels squishy when you touch it.

This *cephalohematoma* is really just a large bruise made of fluid and blood which collects between the scalp and the skull. It may take weeks, months, or—in rare cases—years to completely disappear. As time goes by, you may feel a firm ring or ridge around the edge, which gradually closes in.

If the bump is extremely large, especially if your baby had a difficult birth, your pediatrician may order a skull x-ray to see if there is a fracture underneath. Even if there is, most of the time nothing is done about it except to make sure your child's head grows normally over the first few months.

♥ IT IS NORMAL

- to feel a soft bump on the side of the head for weeks after birth.

☎ CALL YOUR PEDIATRICIAN IF

· the bump was not there at birth but you notice it sometime later.

· it seems to hurt the baby when you touch it or there is redness or drainage in the area.

· you see a pimple or sore on the skin overlying the bump.

4	SCALY CRUSTS ON THE SCALP
	(CRADLE CAP)

Some newborns develop greasy-looking, white or brownish scales that stick tightly to the scalp. These scales are not itchy or painful, and mainly just look bad. The same scaly rash may break out on the eyebrows, forehead, and behind the ears.

Your pediatrician can give you specific instructions for reducing the severity of the scaling but it will usually go away on its own by six months even if you do nothing. If cradle cap is severe and does not improve with simple measures, or is not better by six months, it could be due to a rare condition called Histiocytosis X. This is diagnosed by a skin biopsy.

☆ IT IS COMMON FOR

· newborns to have cradle cap.

☎ CALL YOUR PEDIATRICIAN FOR

· instructions on how to control it.

☞ SEE YOUR PEDIATRICIAN FOR

· cradle cap that is severe, extends beyond the scalp, or will not improve with simple treatment by age six months.

5 | PIMPLES ON THE FACE, FOREHEAD, NECK, AND SHOULDERS (INFANT ACNE)

Around one month red bumps with a small amount of yellow or white material appear on the face and may spread to the rest of the head, the neck, or the shoulders. Although this outbreak often looks worse when the baby has been warm, such as after a nap or a bout of crying, it is not strictly speaking a heat rash.

It is called "infant acne" because it resembles the pimples of adolescent acne.

As far as I know, nobody has studied whether babies who have acne as newborns are more likely to have it as teenagers. I do know, however, that it always seems to be at its worst just when relatives come over to see the new baby or right at the time you plan to have a picture taken.

There is no treatment for infant acne except time. It will go away in a month or two and will leave no scars.

♥ IT IS NORMAL

· to have acne on the face and chest from one month until two or three months of age.

☎ CALL YOUR PEDIATRICIAN IF

· the pimples are not small and firm and are not confined to the head and shoulders. Loose, large yellow blisters or pimples elsewhere on your baby's body may mean there is a skin infection, which should be treated promptly with antibiotics.

6 | SPITTING UP FOOD OR BLOOD

A little spitting up is normal. Formula-fed babies spit up material that looks like cottage cheese, while breast-fed babies spit up a thin, milky liquid. One of the many arguments in favor of breastfeeding, by the way, is that spit-up breast milk smells better and stains less than spit-up formula.

It is also not uncommon for babies to spit up occasionally through the nose as well as the mouth.

You may understandably be worried if your baby spits up some bright red or brown blood along with the milk, but if you are breastfeeding there may be no cause for alarm. Check your nipples for cracks. Most of the time, an otherwise healthy breastfeeding infant who spits up a little blood has swallowed it from mother's bleeding nipple. Blood irritates the stomach and is usually vomited. If you don't see or feel a crack, express a little milk to see if it is blood-tinged.

If you find blood on your nipple or in your breast milk, give your baby plain water or sugar water for one feeding to clear the rest of the blood from the stomach. Then avoid using the cracked nipple for a few feedings to give it a chance to heal. A nipple shield—which you can get at most pharmacies or from your local La Leche League—avoids irritation to a healing nipple while still allowing the baby to feed from that breast.

Swallowed blood may pass through the intestinal tract of a newborn with little change, so you might see some blood mixed with stool as well.

If you see no evidence of blood from your nipple, if your baby is formula-fed, or if there is more than just a little bit of blood, your baby should be examined promptly.

♥ IT IS NORMAL FOR

- babies to spit up occasionally.
- breastfed babies to vomit a small amount of blood from their mother's cracked nipple.
- babies to spit up through their nose once in a while.

☎ CALL YOUR PEDIATRICIAN IF

- spitting up is forceful and constant.
- spit-up *persistently* comes through the nose—

this can be a sign of a defect in the roof of the mouth, which may not be easily visible on routine examination.

- your baby spits up blood and
- you do not find a source of bleeding from your nipples,
- your baby is formula-fed, or
- the amount of blood is more than a small spot.

7 | BREAST LUMP WITH
OR WITHOUT DISCHARGE

Female hormones which stimulate a mother's breasts to enlarge and produce milk are transferred from mother to baby during pregnancy, so many babies—male as well as female—are born with lumps of enlarged breast tissue underneath their nipples. In some babies this is no more than a little nubbin on one side that can be felt but not seen, while other babies may have large lumpy breasts on one or both sides.

Breast lumps do not occur in premature babies; in fact, they are one of the signs your pediatrician looks for on the first examination after birth to make sure your baby was born at full term.

Large swollen breasts may release a drop or two of whitish, watery liquid when gently squeezed. The larger the breast lump, the more likely there is to be some discharge. About one in twenty term babies has this milky fluid.

In the seventeenth century it was thought that if this "witch's milk" was not squeezed from the breasts regularly, it would be stolen by witches and goblins and used in casting spells. Not only is this obviously not true, but you can cause problems by repeatedly and vigorously irritating this delicate tissue.

♥ IT IS NORMAL FOR

   • your full-term baby to have breast lumps and discharge for about two months after birth.

☎ CALL YOUR PEDIATRICIAN IF

   • there is any redness around the nipple or the discharge looks like pus or blood. On rare occasions breast lumps can become infected.

8	HICCUPS

Most babies hiccup now and again, perhaps because swallowed air in the stomach pushes up on the diaphragm. You do not need to do anything about it, and hiccups will stop on their own.

♥ IT IS NORMAL FOR

   • babies to get hiccups frequently.

9	IRREGULAR BREATHING

Except for times when your baby is in deepest sleep, breathing is rarely regular and even. When your baby is excited and active, rapid, shallow breaths with occasional loud inhalations are normal. At rest, you may note periods of rapid breathing alternating irregularly with deeper, slower breaths.

♥ IT IS NORMAL FOR

   • your baby to breathe irregularly.

☎ CALL YOUR PEDIATRICIAN IF

   • breathing is interrupted by several seconds of no breath at all, especially during sleep.
   • your baby's lips or face turn blue or pale during periods of slow or no breathing.

• you notice the chest sinking in when your baby breathes.

☎ CALL YOUR PEDIATRICIAN OR GO TO AN EMERGENCY ROOM *IMMEDIATELY* IF

• breathing is *rapid (more than forty breaths per minute) or associated with a grunting ("uh") or groaning sound. This can be a sign of serious medical problems and should be evaluated immediately.*

| 10 | PROTRUDING BREASTBONE |

The chest cavities of newborns are much smaller than their abdominal cavities. In fact, you can't help but notice how that sweet little belly sticks out farther than the chest, especially after eating. The tip of the breastbone, called the xiphoid process, is a small triangle of bone that is not tightly anchored to the rib cage. It often sticks out just where the chest meets the bulging stomach.

This bone eventually flattens out as your baby becomes a toddler.

♥ IT IS NORMAL FOR

• the tip of the breastbone to protrude.

☎ CALL YOUR PEDIATRICIAN IF

• you notice that the chest is asymmetrical—bulging on one side or sinking in on the other. This may be a sign of an underlying abnormality of the ribs, lungs, or heart.

| 11 | JITTERS AND TWITCHES |

Newborns make all sorts of seemingly random movements, some of which are trembly or jittery. Smaller newborns and premature babies have more of these movements than larger, more mature babies. In the newborn nursery, your pediatrician may check your baby for low blood sugar, low calcium, or some other medical problems. Most of the time, however, this is merely due to an immaturity of the nervous system.

During the first weeks, your baby should startle at a sudden movement or a loud noise. When infants are startled, they open their eyes widely, raise their hands, and bring them somewhat jerkily together over their head. This normal response, called the Moro Reflex, disappears after the first month.

♥ IT IS NORMAL FOR
   · newborns to tremble and shake for a second or two when startled.

☎ CALL YOUR PEDIATRICIAN IF
   · there are abnormal eye movements associated with the trembling.
   · movements are jerky, irregular, and not associated with a noise or movement.
   · trembling lasts more than a second or two.
   · movements do not quiet down with holding or swaddling.

| 12 | BLUE HANDS AND FEET |

Immediately after birth virtually every full-term newborn develops blue hands and feet because the outside world is so much colder than the comfy, body-temperature amniotic fluid inside the womb. One of the reasons your baby might have been placed under an overhead warmer in the delivery room when not in your arms was to minimize the stress of this drop in temperature.

It can take as long as several hours for the initial

blueness to disappear, and you may notice that it reappears from time to time when your baby is being changed or bathed.

Also, in the first few weeks, you may notice that your baby's legs turn a deep blue when the baby is held upright. This should clear up once the baby is laid down again.

♥ IT IS NORMAL FOR

- newborns to have blue hands and feet.

☎ CALL YOUR PEDIATRICIAN IF

- you notice blueness of the lips.
- blue hands and feet remain even when the baby is warm.
- blue legs persist after the baby lies down.

| 13 | YELLOW DISCHARGE OR SWELLING OF THE CIRCUMCISION |

After surgical removal of the foreskin, known as circumcision, a freshly circumcised penis is immediately wrapped in a diaper into which the baby urinates and defecates—hardly the best environment for healing. Therefore, the penis can look pretty strange even when healing normally.

If the circumcision was done with a clear plastic ring held on with a string, you may see blackened tissue around the outside edge of the string and a slight swelling at the inside edge. The ring should fall off within ten days.

If no plastic ring was used, the end of the penis will probably be red for a few days with a small amount of yellowish material adhering firmly to it. If there is no swelling and the baby is comfortable and urinating well, just wait for this to clear up on its own. Sometimes leaving the diaper off for a few hours every day—taking appropriate precautions for squirts, of course—may speed healing.

♥ IT IS NORMAL FOR NEWBORN BOYS TO
* have a little swelling at the edge of the plastic ring.
* form a little blackened tissue around the string.
* ooze yellowish material which dries on the end of the penis or develop redness on the end of the penis.

☎ CALL YOUR PEDIATRICIAN IF
* urine comes out in little dribbles or in less than a good stream.
* your newborn strains with urination.
* the head of the penis is dark blue or black.
* there is more pus oozing than just the little bit described above.
* you see more than a few drops of blood on the diaper once in a while.
* there is significant swelling or redness of the penis or the skin around it.
* the ring does not fall off in fourteen days.
* your baby acts sick in any way.

| 14 | MARBLED SKIN |

When older children and adults are cold, they conserve their body heat by shivering and developing goose bumps, but newborns cannot do this. The only way they can preserve heat is to pull back the blood vessels near the surface of the skin. When they do that, their hands and feet turn blue, and the skin on the arms, legs, and trunk appears mottled or marbled.

This usually goes away once the baby is warm.

♥ IT IS NORMAL FOR
* newborns to have marbled or mottled looking skin when they are cold.

☞ CALL IT TO YOUR PEDIATRICIAN'S ATTENTION IF

• an area of skin appears marbled all the time. This may be a sign of an abnormal formation of blood vessels under the skin.

☎ CALL YOUR PEDIATRICIAN *IMMEDIATELY* IF

• mottling occurs with sweating, fever, or any other sign that your baby might be sick; this could mean a serious medical emergency.

| 15 | YELLOW SKIN AND EYES (JAUNDICE) |

Approximately 10 percent of all healthy term newborns and an even higher proportion of premature babies develop jaundice, a yellow discoloration of the skin and the whites of the eyes. In older infants or children, jaundice is always a sign that there is something wrong—hepatitis, for example. In newborns, however, it is not usually a sign of serious disease.

Jaundice might result because the baby was born with too many red blood cells, or develops mild dehydration because of too little fluid intake in the first few days of life when mother's breast milk is not yet flowing in sufficient quantity. Possible medical causes of jaundice, which are much less common, are blood group incompatibility between mother and baby, infection, and liver abnormalities.

Your pediatrician will decide what is the likeliest cause based on a combination of blood tests, birth history, and physical examination.

The yellow pigment that causes jaundice is called bilirubin. If bilirubin in the blood rises to a very high level, there is a slight chance of brain damage. Therefore, pediatricians do not allow the level to become high enough to endanger the baby. Before it reaches the danger stage, newborns are placed under a special light that breaks down bilirubin through the skin into a harmless by-product that is excreted through the kidneys.

Breastfed babies may remain slightly jaundiced for as long as six weeks. The cause for this is obscure— perhaps there is some naturally occurring substance in mother's milk. At any rate, it is normal and not a reason to stop nursing. Sometimes a drop in jaundice after 8-12 hours off the breast is enough to prove the cause, and breastfeeding can be resumed.

♥ IT IS NORMAL FOR

•   newborns to have mild jaundice for as long as four to six weeks after birth, especially if they are breastfed.

☎ CALL YOUR PEDIATRICIAN IF

•   jaundice was not there at two to three days of age but you noticed it sometime later.

•   jaundice appears to be deepening in color.

•   your baby is acting sick, feeding poorly, or has a fever over 100°F.

| 16 | PINK PATCHES ON THE EYELIDS, |
| | FOREHEAD, AND NECK |

Known as "angel kisses" or "stork bites," these flat, red, or salmon pink patches turn pale when you press on them and may turn more deeply red when your baby cries. They are more common in white babies, although they can be seen in Asians and blacks as well. They start to fade at about six months and are usually gone from the face by one year, a little later for ones on the back of the neck.

In a few light-complexioned people these areas may remain visible into adulthood, especially when they become angry or upset.

♥ IT IS NORMAL FOR NEWBORNS TO

•   have salmon-colored patches on the forehead, eyelids, and the nape of the neck.

17 | STEAMY-LOOKING EYE; MUCUS
OR EYELASHES IN THE EYE

If I had a little bit of mucus, blanket fuzz, or an eyelash swimming around on the surface of my eye, it would drive me crazy, but those things do not seem to affect infants. There is no need to do anything about a little fuzz or a hair if your baby is comfortable—the natural flow of tears and blinking will clear the eye.

On the other hand, if you see haziness or a steamy film over the colored part of the eye, especially if one eye appears large compared to the other, your baby may have congenital glaucoma—increased pressure in the eye.

If left untreated, congenital glaucoma can lead to blindness. The sooner your pediatrician diagnoses this possibility and refers you to an opthalmologist, the more likely it is that normal vision will be preserved. The cloudiness may come and go, so see your pediatrician even if you are not sure.

Cloudiness or discoloration of the pupil, the dark spot in the center of the eye, can be caused by a congenital cataract or tumor. These also must be treated as soon as possible.

If mucus collects on the inner corner of one or both of your baby's eyes without any swelling or redness, a tear duct may be blocked. Often there is an overflow of tears, but not always. This common condition almost always clears up before age one, but sometimes the duct must be opened by an opthalmologist.

♥ IT IS NORMAL FOR NEWBORNS TO

· have mucus or an eyelash swimming around on the surface of the eye.

☎ CALL YOUR PEDIATRICIAN IF

· you notice any haziness to the eye, even if it comes and goes, or discoloration of the pupil.

- yellow mucus or pus collects in the inner corner of an eye.
- one eye seems larger than the other.

18 | STUFFY NOSE, NOISY BREATHING

At first, newborns can breathe only through their nose, not through their mouth. Not until after the first month or two do they learn to alternate breathing between nose and mouth. This is handy because while they learn to eat there is less danger of choking.

Since babies must breathe through their nose and cannot sniffle or blow, any mucus or swelling of the lining of the nose causes snorting, sneezing, gurgling, and other musical sounds. New parents often think that this means their newborn has a cold, but usually that is incorrect.

If your baby is sleeping and eating well and has no cough or fever, there is no need to worry. If the stuffy nose is accompanied by irritability, fever, poor feeding, or any other signs of illness, on the other hand—especially if someone in your household has a cold—you may need to see your pediatrician.

♥ IT IS NORMAL FOR NEWBORNS TO
- have mucus in their noses.
- breathe noisily.
- sneeze.

☎ CALL YOUR PEDIATRICIAN IF
- your baby has any signs of illness, other than a stuffy nose, such as irritability or a temperature over 100.5°F.
- the stuffiness is interrupting sleep or feeding.
- stuffiness is accompanied by yellow or green discharge from the nose.

19 | BLUE SPOTS ON THE TRUNK AND BUTTOCKS

Dark-skinned babies such as black, American or East Indian, Mediterranean, Asian, or Central American children often have large, flat blue spots on the trunk and buttocks. Known as "Mongolian spots," they usually disappear in a few years, although they can sometimes persist into adulthood.

Mongolian spots look an awful lot like bruises, and people who are not familiar with these birthmarks might mistake them for signs of child abuse. Most doctors are familiar with them, however.

♥ IT IS NORMAL FOR
  • newborns to have Mongolian spots on their trunks or buttocks at birth.

☎ CALL YOUR PEDIATRICIAN IF
  • you notice bruiselike marks appearing *after* birth.

20 | TINY PIT AT THE BASE OF THE SPINE

While your baby is still a microscopic embryo, the spinal cord and vertebrae start forming from the middle of the back outward toward the head and buttocks. Sometimes a small pit remains at the bottom of the backbone. This is usually of no concern. If, however, there is any drainage, if there is hair growing out of it, a lump near or under it, or if the crease between the buttocks is crooked below it, be sure to bring it to your pediatrician's attention. There may be an underlying malformation of the end of the spinal cord which should be investigated and corrected as soon as possible.

♥ IT IS NORMAL FOR
- newborns to have a small pit at the base of the spine.

☎ CALL YOUR PEDIATRICIAN IF
- there is any drainage of clear or cloudy fluid.
- there are hairs growing from the pit.
- there is a lump near or under the pit.
- the skin is discolored around or near it.

21 | RAISED, RED SPOTS ON THE SKIN

Many of the spots we call "birthmarks" are not really present at birth. Bright red spots with an irregular or bumpy surface, called "strawberry marks," can appear anywhere on your baby's body in the first weeks after birth and can vary in size from a pinhead to several inches.

Almost all of these eventually disappear. Even if a strawberry mark is disfiguring, most pediatricians, dermatologists and plastic surgeons will urge you to wait until age four or so to see if it goes away by itself. If treatment is necessary, such as when a large strawberry mark on an eyelid interferes with vision because it overlaps the eyelid, laser therapy is the current choice.

♥ IT IS NORMAL FOR
- newborns to develop strawberry marks in the weeks after birth.

☎ CALL YOUR PEDIATRICIAN IF
- you notice many red spots forming.
- the red spots are accompanied by bruising.

| 22 | GREEN STOOL |

A newborn's stool is normally sticky and black the first day or two of life. After that it turns yellow if the baby is breastfed, brown if formula-fed. Once in a while you may see a bright green stool.

Green stools probably happen because the liver produces a little bit more bile, or sometimes a particular brand of formula is responsible. Babies with intestinal infections may have green stools, but there usually are other signs of illness such as diarrhea, fever, etc.

Whatever the reason, there is no need to make any dietary changes if your baby is otherwise well; it is a common occurrence.

♥ IT IS NORMAL FOR
- newborns to have a green stool now and then.

☎ CALL YOUR PEDIATRICIAN IF
- the stool is red at any time or tarry black after the first few days or if it is chalky white.
- green stool is accompanied by any signs of illness.

| 23 | SOFT OR WATERY STOOL |

Breastfed babies may have one stool every few days or a small stool with every feeding. No matter how many stools are normal for your baby, they usually are a little loose and watery, sometimes squirting out. This does not mean the baby has diarrhea.

Formula-fed babies develop firmer stools after the first week or so, but breastfed babies should always have loose ones.

♥ IT IS NORMAL FOR

· newborns to have loose, watery stools with a little seedy, yellow material mixed in.

☎ CALL YOUR PEDIATRICIAN IF

· your formula-fed baby used to have firm stools but now has frequent, loose stools.

· loose stools are accompanied by vomiting.

· the normal loose, watery stool of your breastfed baby turns hard and dry.

| 24 | VAGINAL BLOOD OR MUCUS |

The vaginas of newborn girls normally produce clear or milky white mucus on and off during the first weeks. You need only wipe it away with a moist cotton ball. Do not scrub the delicate vaginal tissues vigorously.

This discharge is the result of hormones in the baby's bloodstream which came from mother—the same hormones that cause breast swelling (see Number 7, page 27). When the level of these hormones in the bloodstream decreases a few days after birth, "withdrawal bleeding," a condition similar to a period, may occur. A little bright red blood appears on the diaper mixed with mucus.

If there is only a little blood and it stops right away, there is no need to do anything. If bleeding continues, however, there may be a problem with blood clotting, a polyp, or some other abnormality in the genital tract.

♥ IT IS NORMAL FOR

· newborn females to have mucus and sometimes even a little bright red blood from the vagina during the first week or two.

☎ CALL YOUR PEDIATRICIAN IF
- the bleeding continues or is more than a little spot.
- mucus becomes yellow, green or foul-smelling.

---

25 | STRAINING AT STOOL

At first, the only way you know when your baby has had a bowel movement is when you find it in the diaper. Newborns pass their first stools with a minimum of fanfare. As the weeks wear on they begin to participate more and more, grunting, straining, and turning red before the stool comes out.

If your baby is grunting and straining but the stool that comes out is soft, there is no need to do anything but wait for practice to make it easier for your baby to pass a stool. Straining is not necessarily a sign of constipation.

Constipation means the difficult passage of infrequent, hard stools. Breastfed babies should never be constipated; although they may have only one stool a week, it should be soft. Formula-fed babies may develop constipation from certain formulas.

Make sure your baby is straining to produce stool and not urine; straining with stool is normal, straining with urination is not.

♥ IT IS NORMAL FOR
- babies to strain, grunt, cry, and turn red when passing a stool.

☎ CALL YOUR PEDIATRICIAN IF
- stools are hard and difficult to pass.
- straining occurs with urination, not defecation.
- your baby strains frequently but produces stool infrequently.

26 | STRAINING DURING URINATION

While straining at stool may be normal, straining with urination is not. Malformed structures in and around the bladder can make passing urine difficult. Sometimes the urinary stream in boys will also be weak or dribbling rather than the usual little fountain, but not always.

If you notice your baby straining with urination, bring it to your pediatrician's attention at once. Early detection and correction of an obstruction to urine flow can preserve kidney function.

⊗ IT IS **NOT** NORMAL FOR

- infants to strain while urinating.

☎ CALL YOUR PEDIATRICIAN IF

- you notice your baby straining while urinating.
- the urinary stream is weak and dribbling.

27 | PINK-COLORED URINE

During the first week or two, some babies excrete a chemical in their urine which stains diapers a soft pink. This is not the same color as blood, but is is reasonable for you to think it might be at first. Usually this only happens once or twice and never appears again.

♥ IT IS NORMAL FOR

- newborns to have a pink color to their urine once or twice.

☎ CALL YOUR PEDIATRICIAN

- if this persists or if it looks like blood. Bring in the stained diaper. There is a simple test for blood that your doctor can do right on the diaper immediately.

28 | CLEAR BEADS OR GRANULES ON THE DIAPER

A few years ago this caused considerable consternation until we all figured out what it was. In some of the superabsorbent disposable diapers, a gel that absorbs urine may leak onto the surface of the diaper and deposit tiny clear or whitish granules which look as though they have come from the baby's urine.

This material is not harmful and you need do nothing about it.

♥ IT IS NORMAL FOR
 • a little clear, granular material to ooze from a superabsorbent diaper.

29 | BOWED LEGS AND CURVED FEET

My father used to love to tell a story about my uncle seeing me for the first time shortly after I was born. A look of horror spread over his face and he said, "Her legs are crooked!"

Infants have to fold up substantially in order to fit into a uterus, so their legs are usually crossed over each other and over the baby's belly. In the process, an inward bend to the legs and feet results.

This bend to the legs almost always straightens out in the first few weeks, although a slight bowing to the legs can be normal even through toddlerhood.

Sometimes the feet were so tightly folded in the uterus that there is a crease across the instep and the front part of the foot curves so far inward that gentle pressure cannot straighten the foot. In that case, special shoes or even a small cast for a few weeks may be necessary.

♥ IT IS NORMAL FOR
· newborns to have bowed legs and in-curving feet.

☞ BRING IT TO YOUR PEDIATRICIAN'S ATTENTION
· if the curve seems excessive, especially in the feet.

| 30 | OOZING BELLY BUTTON |

As the tissue of the umbilical stump starts to decay, it usually dries up and falls off neatly. Sometimes, however, it stays soft, oozes, and smells terrible.

Before seeing your doctor, try getting some peroxide or alcohol way down under the stump by moving it a little to the side or picking it up gently. Also, leave the belly button open to the air for a few hours each day. If that doesn't work, your pediatrician can cauterize it with a little silver nitrate and it will dry up in a jiffy.

♥ IT IS NORMAL FOR
· belly buttons to get smelly and oozy.

☎ CALL YOUR PEDIATRICIAN IF
· leaving it open to the air and dousing it with alcohol does not solve the problem.

☎ CALL YOUR PEDIATRICIAN *IMMEDIATELY* IF
· there is any redness to the skin around the belly button. This could mean a potentially serious infection.

| 31 | INGROWN TOENAILS |

There is a minor design flaw in even the most perfect baby. For some reason, their soft toenails can grow crookedly and the edge of the nail can irritate the surrounding skin.

If you notice the corner of the nail on the big toe start to turn red or collect a little yellow material, put some antibiotic ointment on a Band-Aid and keep the toe covered for a few days in socks or pajamas with feet. Usually that is enough to relieve the irritation and allow the nail to grow out.

♥ IT IS NORMAL FOR
· newborns to have mild ingrown toenails once in a while.

☞ SEE YOUR PEDIATRICIAN IF
· the area looks infected or the toe is swollen.
· if the simple remedies above do not clear it up in a few days.

| 32 | FEVER |

Newborns have a limited ability to fight infections so what might be a minor illness in an older child can be a dangerous one in a newborn. For that reason, any fever over 100.5°F in a newborn should be treated as though there is a serious infection until proven otherwise. If treatment is delayed until a newborn acts really sick, precious time will have been lost.

(*Note:* A sick newborn may also have an abnormally *low* temperature.)

If there is a cold running through your family and your pediatrician feels strongly that your baby has the family virus, you may be told to go home but to keep in close contact every few hours. In many cases, however, a newborn with a fever will at least have some blood tests, a urinalysis, perhaps a chest x-ray, and even a spinal tap. Your pediatrician may even want to hospitalize your baby for a day or two for precautionary treatment until cultures are completed and your baby is all right.

⊗ IT IS **NOT** NORMAL FOR

• newborn infants to have a fever.

☎ CALL YOUR PEDIATRICIAN **IMMEDIATELY**

• if your newborn (up to age two months) has a temperature over 100.5°F.

• your baby is acting sick and her temperature is *under* 97.5°F.

See the Chapter IX, "Fever," for more details.

| 33 | VOMITING |

Spitting up is normal, vomiting is not. The distinction between the two is not always so obvious, however. Sometimes it is hard to tell one from the other. The major difference is force and quantity. Vomiting means forceful ejection of most or all of the stomach contents; spitting up is gentler and smaller in quantity.

It does not make any difference whether what is spit up is curdled or not. Milk curdles when it reacts with acid in the stomach. If milk hasn't stayed long enough in the stomach, it won't be curdled yet; if it was there for a while, it will be.

Forceful, "projectile" vomiting, when stomach contents are shot several feet from the baby, can be perfectly normal if it happens only from time to time. Persistent projectile vomiting, however, especially at about four weeks of age, might be due to an overgrowth of the muscle at the end of the stomach, called *pyloric stenosis*. It is more common in males than females and often runs in families. Characteristically, the baby will be hungry right after vomiting and want to feed again right away.

Vomiting beginning in the first days or weeks of life can signal serious problems such as an obstruction in the gastrointestinal tract or an infection. Babies who are fed formula, however, may vomit merely because of difficulty digesting a particular formula. There usually

are other symptoms of formula intolerance such as abdominal pain, excessive gas, or diarrhea, but sometimes
vomiting is the only sign.

♥ IT IS NORMAL FOR

• newborns to spit up or vomit now and then. It
is even normal to have projectile vomiting once in a
while.

☎ CALL YOUR PEDIATRICIAN IF

• the vomiting happens more than once a day or
occurs frequently over several days.

☞ SEE YOUR PEDIATRICIAN *IMMEDIATELY* IF

• projectile vomiting persists.
• your baby does not seem to be keeping anything
down.
• your baby looks sick, she has poor color, the
vomiting is associated with a fever over 100.5°F, or there
are any other signs of illness.

CHAPTER II

Head, Eyes, Ears, Nose, & Throat

| 1 | **HEAD** |

A. Headache

Most adults take headaches in their stride. When children complain of headache, though, parents tend to think that there must be something seriously wrong—eyestrain at least, or even a brain tumor.

Actually, headaches are more common in children than most adults realize. Studies show that anywhere from 20 to 50 percent of children experience headaches during school years, and as many as 10 percent suffer from some form of migraine. There are many causes for headaches, and if your child complains frequently, seek the help of your pediatrician to figure out what is causing them.

i. Minor, Occasional

Viral infections and fevers cause headaches which go away when the fever decreases and the infection clears. Some children (and adults, including me) get headaches when they are hungry.

Headaches caused by food are sometimes hard to diagnose because the reaction may come two or three days after the food is eaten. MSG, nitrites and some other food additives, milk, and caffeine are possible culprits. One of my patients had "peanut butter" headaches, although I have never seen that before or since. He had a headache every day after lunch during math class, and I was sure it was due to tension because he was having difficulty with math. Then I found out that he ate peanut butter sandwiches for lunch every school day. When his mother stopped sending peanut butter sandwiches in his lunch bag, the headaches stopped.

ii. Tension

Tension is far and away the most common cause of recurrent headaches in children. Worries over school, parental divorce, even excitement about an upcoming event can cause tightening of the neck muscles that can lead to a headache.

Tension headaches usually hurt both sides of the head, involving both temples and the forehead or spreading across the back of the head. Pain is equal on both sides, in contrast to migraine, which is often on one side only. It is difficult to fall asleep with a tension headache, but lying down in a dark, quiet room after taking pain medication often helps.

iii. Migraine

Migraine headaches occur periodically but not necessarily regularly; are associated with abdominal pain, nausea, or vomiting; are usually only on one side of the head; and are relieved by sleep. At the onset of a headache, children might complain of sparkling lights or black spots. Some children have transitory numbness or even temporary paralysis of an arm or hand.

Migraines run in families. About 90 percent of children with migraine headaches have a relative in their immediate family who also has had them.

Many children with migraine have been troubled by car sickness before their headaches appear.

> *iv. Other Causes of Headaches* (and these are not the only ones) include:

> Disorders of the jaw joint (TMJ, or temporo-mandibular joint)
> Excessive vitamin intake
> Carbon monoxide poisoning from a gas leak
> Depression
> Sinus infections
> Head injury
> Acute glaucoma (increased pressure in the eye)
> Eyestrain (this is only rarely a cause in children)

For an occasional headache that is not severe, simple pain medication such as acetaminophen (Tylenol, Liquiprin, Tempra, etc.) and a brief rest in a quiet, darkened room are usually sufficient. For severe or frequent headaches, see your pediatrician.

♥ IT IS NORMAL FOR

· school-aged children to have headaches once in a while, especially at times of stress or with minor illness.

· children to vomit once or twice with migraine headaches and then sleep for a few hours.

· children prone to motion sickness to develop migraine headaches.

☎ CALL YOUR PEDIATRICIAN *IMMEDIATELY* IF

· headaches occur in a child under six.

· headache follows a head injury.

· the pain is severe—your child is writhing or screaming.

• your child is acting abnormally—confused, walking unsteadily, slurring speech, for example.

• your child vomits more than once.

• your child's neck is stiff.

• the pain becomes worse and worse despite pain-relieving measures, or the headache lasts more than twelve hours.

• the onset of pain was sudden and severe or pain was brought on by a sneeze or cough.

• your child does not want to be moved.

• one pupil is noticeably larger than the other.

• the headaches are worst in the morning or there is morning vomiting.

☞ MAKE AN APPOINTMENT WITH YOUR PEDIATRICIAN IF

• headaches are frequent and interfere with school or other activities.

• the pain is restricted to one side of the head all the time.

• there is any other reason you are worried about your child.

B. Lumps on the Back of the Head

When you brush or shampoo your child's hair or stroke the back of your child's head affectionately, you may feel small hard lumps from the size of a pea to the size of walnuts at the base of the skull. These are lymph nodes or "glands," the same kind of tissue that swells in the neck with a sore throat.

Enlarged nodes appear here especially after chicken pox when there have been pocks on the scalp, or after a rash or infection on the scalp. Some viral infections such as roseola and German Measles are particularly prone to swell the nodes in the back of the head.

Sometimes children develop these enlarged nodes without any signs of infection or irritation.

If the lumps you feel are not tender, red, or very large, you need only keep an eye on them for a few weeks to see if they go away. Nodes that are tender or red may contain a bacterial infection and should be treated with antibiotics. It is *extremely rare* that lumps like this in children are cancerous.

♥ IT IS NORMAL FOR

•   children to have enlarged lymph nodes on the back of the head after some infections or even for no discernible reason.

☎ CALL YOUR PEDIATRICIAN IF

•   the lumps are very large, red, or tender.

•   the lumps do not start to shrink in three to four weeks.

C. Tilted Head

Small children do not complain about problems with their vision, but instead try to adapt to them. When a child holds his head or face in an abnormal position, he may be compensating for a visual imbalance. If his eyes are not aligned evenly, tilting the head can correct double vision. If the head tilt is present for that reason, the tilt goes away during sleep.

A persistent head tilt may also be the result of tightness of one neck muscle. In these cases, it is usually present from birth or shortly after and your child will keep the head tilted all the time, including during sleep.

⊗ IT IS *NOT* NORMAL FOR

•   children to keep their head tilted.

☎ CALL YOUR PEDIATRICIAN FOR

•   any head tilt.

D. Dandruff

Regular, adult-type dandruff is unusual in children. Sometimes dry, scaling scalp is related to eczema or seborrhea elsewhere on the child's body, or comes from dryness after frequent shampooing or sun and wind exposure. However, a mild infection of the scalp caused by a fungus related to the one that causes ring-worm may be implicated in many cases of stubborn childhood "dandruff."

If what appears to be dandruff on your child's scalp does not respond to simple treatment with anti-eczema medications or dandruff shampoos, see your pediatrician. A scraping from the scalp may reveal the true cause.

⊗ IT IS **NOT** NORMAL FOR

· children to have dandruff.

☞ SEE YOUR PEDIATRICIAN IF

· scaly, dry scalp does not respond to simple remedies.

| 2 | EARS |

A. Earache

i. *Middle Ear Infection*

At least one out of three children will have had at least one middle ear infection by the age of three. They are most common between six months and two years, but continue to plague children frequently up to age ten.

Suspect an ear infection if your infant is irritable a few days after the onset of a cold. Pressure in the middle ear increases when children are lying down so your infant or toddler may be fine while awake but unhappy after going down for a nap or to sleep for the night. Infants and toddlers might hit or pull their ear or stick a finger into it. An older child can tell you the ear hurts or that there is a "noise" or a "bug" in the ear. One of my five-year-old patients marched into my office with a Band-Aid stuck carefully across the ear. I did not have to ask him what the problem was.

Middle ear infections come from congestion inside the ear, not from wind or water getting in from outside. They usually follow a cold. You are not responsible for an ear infection if you did not put a hat on your child on a windy day or allowed bathwater to get into the ear. Do not, however, ever let your baby drink a bottle or nurse lying down flat. That *can* irritate the inside opening to the middle ear and either cause or prolong infections.

Colds are contagious, but ear infections are not. The chances of suffering from an ear infection are increased if your child attends group day-care (because of the increased number of colds), is bottle-fed, or lives in a household with a smoker because exposure to smoke makes colds more prolonged and more severe.

Middle ear infection needs prompt medical treatment. To relieve pain temporarily during the night, however, try:

· acetaminophen by mouth.

· a warm compress—either a warm washcloth, a hot water bottle, or a heating pad on low.

WARNING: Never allow your child to sleep with a heating pad; children's tender skin can burn easily, even on a low setting.

· an ice bag or ice in a washcloth for twenty minutes each hour (if heat seems to make the pain worse).

· a few drops of warmed-up oil—olive, mineral, or baby oil—if there is no drainage from the ear. Put a small amount in a glass and let it stand in a container of hot water for a few minutes. Do not heat the oil in the microwave or it will be too hot. Put a few drops into the painful ear, and seal it with a wad of cotton.

ii. Swimmer's Ear

While middle ear infections are more frequent during colder seasons, outer ear infection, or *swimmer's ear*, occurs mostly during the summer months when children swim (or even throughout the year if your child is on a swim team).

Swimmer's ear hurts when you tug on the ear or touch the area around it. The ear itself or the area in front of it may appear swollen and there might be a white, cheeselike, or green discharge.

Swimmer's ear needs prompt medical attention. To relieve pain temporarily during the night, however, try:
- acetaminophen by mouth.
- a hot water bottle, a warm compress, or ice—whichever gives the most relief.

iii. TMJ

A rare but sometimes baffling cause for what appears to be ear pain is really a spasm or inflammation of the jaw joint just in front of the ear (the TMJ, or temporomandibular joint). Although more common in teenagers and adults, children can suffer from this also. If ear pain persists and your pediatrician cannot find any evidence of ear disease, see a dentist or head and neck surgeon who is knowledgeable about TMJ problems.

♥ IT IS NORMAL FOR
- children to develop ear infections after a cold. They are especially prone if they are bottle-fed, live in a house with tobacco smoke, or are in group day-care.
- the pain to be severe, especially at night, when lying down, or after coming in from the cold.

☞ SEE YOUR PEDIATRICIAN IF
- your child complains of any ear pain.

☎ CALL YOUR PEDIATRICIAN *IMMEDIATELY* IF
- simple pain-relieving measures fail. You may need a stronger medication to get through the night.
- your child's neck is stiff.
- your child walks unsteadily.
- there was a head injury shortly before the ear pain began.

· there is a high fever and your child is acting very sick.

B. Ear Discharge

Whenever anything is draining from your child's ear, do not pack the ear with cotton but allow it to drain freely, and do not use drops of any kind without checking with your pediatrician first.

i. Brown or Reddish-Brown Discharge is usually just ear wax. Some people make dry, flaky wax and others make moist, sticky wax. If there is no pain or fever, merely wipe away what you can see. Sometimes a middle ear infection creates heat around the eardrum that melts the wax, and it drains out as a gush of semi-liquid reddish-brown discharge.

ii. Clear, Watery Discharge could be tears or bathwater draining out. If clear drainage follows a head injury, however, it could signal a fracture at the base of the skull. In that case, see your pediatrician immediately.

iii. Cloudy or Yellow Discharge may come from a middle ear infection which has broken through the eardrum. If there was pain before, the earache suddenly disappears when this happens, but pain does not always precede a ruptured eardrum. Fortunately, although this sounds like it must be a calamitous event, eardrums almost always heal rapidly.

♥ IT IS NORMAL FOR
· children to drain ear wax from time to time.

☎ CALL YOUR PEDIATRICIAN IF
· drainage of ear wax is constant or comes in a sudden rush.
· clear drainage follows a head injury.
· drainage is associated with fever or difficulty walking.
· pus drains from your child's ear.

| 3 | EYES |

A. Red Eyes

The most common reason for red eyes in children is *conjunctivitis*, or *pinkeye*, an infection of the membrane covering the white of the eye. Redness starts at the edges of one or both eyes and gradually imparts a pink color to the whole eye. A little, watery discharge at the beginning may turn into pus. The white may become bumpy or swollen as well as red.

Conjunctivitis can be caused by a virus or bacteria. Viral conjunctivitis usually clears in a few days on its own; bacterial conjunctivitis may need an antibiotic. Usually bacterial conjunctivitis is associated with more pus, redness, and swelling than viral conjunctivitis, but not always. Your pediatrician will probably treat every episode of conjunctivitis with antibiotic eye drops. Whatever the cause, it should be better in two to three days.

If your child has allergies and has an itchy, red eye with little or no discharge, it may be caused by *vernal conjunctivitis,* an allergic reaction to pollen or other irritants in the air. *Tobacco smoke* can also cause these symptoms.

If there is redness near the colored part of the eye (iris), the pupil of the affected eye appears smaller than the other, and especially if there is pain or blurred vision, your child may have *iritis,* an inflammation behind the front of the eye. This is rare in children but it can lead to visual loss if not treated promptly.

A bright red, painless splotch in the white of the eye usually comes from sneezing, coughing, crying hard, vomiting, or a blow to the eye. Even straining with constipation may cause this *subconjunctival hemorrhage,* a sort of bleeding from a broken blood vessel. Many women get these during childbirth, and newborns may have them right after birth.

The bright red spot may take several weeks to clear. As it fades, it changes color just like a bruise, becoming brownish or yellowish before it disappears.

♥ IT IS NORMAL FOR
· a bright red splotch to appear in the white of the eye after a bout of coughing, sneezing, vomiting, or crying.

☎ CALL YOUR PEDIATRICIAN *IMMEDIATELY* IF
· there is redness around the iris, accompanied by pain or blurred vision.
· you notice a difference in the size of the pupils.
· a bright red spot occurs following a blow or other injury to the eye. Your child will need to be checked for other injuries.
· redness is accompanied by pain.

☞ MAKE AN APPOINTMENT WITH YOUR PEDIATRICIAN IF
· there is any redness or infection of the eye.
· there is recurring redness, itching, and/or swelling that may be allergic.

B. Steamy or Milky-Looking Eye

Serious eye problems such as glaucoma (increased pressure in the eye from obstruction to the normal flow of fluid) or a cataract (clouding of the lens) can create a milky or steamy look to the eye. While these ailments are common in older adults, on rare occasions they can appear as congenital problems in infants and children.

In the case of glaucoma, steaminess over the colored part of the eye (the iris) may come and go, and may be so slight that you think you are imagining it at first. Cataracts cause a constant grayish discoloration to the pupil (the black spot in the middle of the colored part of the eye).

All the problems associated with a steamy or milky-looking eye must be corrected immediately in order to preserve vision. If you notice anything, see your pediatrician immediately. If there is cause for concern, you will be referred to a pediatric opthalmologist promptly.

⊗ IT IS *NOT* NORMAL FOR
- children to have a steamy or milky-looking eye.

☎ CALL YOUR PEDIATRICIAN IF
- you notice any clouding or discoloration of the iris or pupil.

C. Crossed Eye, Wandering Eye

Early diagnosis and treatment are important for any crossing or wandering eye. Children's brains compensate for an imbalance in muscle movement or a significant difference in vision by ignoring the signal from the weaker eye. Eventually, this can lead to a loss of vision in that eye (*amblyopia*) through disuse.

Newborn babies cross their eyes often before they learn to focus. If this happens once in a while, it should not worry you. Eyes that cross or wander persistently after two to four months should be examined by a pediatric opthalmologist.

A wandering eye that seems off kilter when looking upward or to one side may not be as threatening to vision, but sometimes needs correction also.

♥ IT IS NORMAL FOR
- children to cross their eyes once in a while up to two months.

☎ CALL YOUR PEDIATRICIAN IF
- crossing persists after two months.
- crossing or wandering eye appears suddenly at any age.

• your baby does not seem to fix on anything but eyes wander all the time.

D. Swollen Eye

The tissues around the eye are soft and loose and can swell quickly and dramatically. Even a simple mosquito bite can create enough swelling to virtually shut the eye. Sometimes a sty begins with general redness and swelling of a lid before it turns into the characteristic "pimple" on the edge of a lid.

Children are particularly susceptible to an infection of the tissues in the eye socket called *orbital cellulitis*—a serious and potentially life-threatening problem. Resembling orbital cellulitis is a slightly less serious infection called *periorbital cellulitis,* which involves the tissues in front of the eye rather than the socket itself.

Both these infections, causing redness and swelling around the eye, are associated with fever and need prompt treatment, sometimes in the hospital. If swelling of the tissues around your child's eye is accompanied by fever, see your pediatrician immediately.

Swelling of the eyelids with no redness or irritation may be caused by fluid retention, perhaps because of kidney problems. If your toddler or preschool-aged child suddenly develops swollen eyes, sudden tightness of belts and waistbands, and puffy feet and hands, the problem may be *nephrotic syndrome,* a kidney disorder that causes protein to leak through the kidneys into the urine.

♥ IT IS NORMAL FOR

• the tissues around the eye to swell dramatically with minor trauma such as an insect bite.

☞ SEE YOUR PEDIATRICIAN *IMMEDIATELY* IF

• there is any redness, tenderness and swelling around the eye, particularly if associated with a fever.

• your child has swollen eyes, hands and feet.

☞ SEE YOUR PEDIATRICIAN IF

·   your child has red, swollen lids with no fever or other signs of illness that does not get better in one day.

| 4 | NOSE |

A. Colds and Runny Noses

Children have an average of six to eight colds per year, but children who are in group day-care, who live in homes with tobacco smoke, and who have allergies suffer from colds more frequently.

Colds are caused by viruses and are spread by contact with infected secretions on hands, toys, and other surfaces. You cannot catch a cold from a draft or by being chilled. Colds are more common in the winter not only because of cold weather but because children are indoors and have closer contact with infected playmates.

It *is* true, however, that some cold and flu viruses seem to disappear during the summer and reappear the next winter. (Where do they go? Probably South America, where it is winter during our summer.)

The usual cold symptoms are runny or stuffy nose, red eyes, sneezing and coughing, and sometimes a fever and sore throat.

There is no cure for a cold. No matter what you do, it will take from five to seven days to run its course. Infants may have mucus problems for two to three weeks afterward. Your pediatrician has no secret prescription, and you are not a negligent parent if you wait a few days before seeing the doctor to see if the cold will get better on its own. If your child develops an ear infection or even pneumonia following a cold, it did not happen because the cold was not treated promptly.

Simple measures such as humidifying indoor air and using acetaminophen for fever and discomfort are enough. Most over-the-counter cold medicines have more side effects for children than benefits. A cough medicine that contains dextromethorphan may help your child sleep at night if coughing interrupts sleep.

♥ IT IS NORMAL FOR

· children to have as many as six or eight colds per year, especially the first year or two they are in day-care.

· children to have a low fever for one to two days at the beginning of a cold.

· a cough and a clear runny nose to last for as long as one to two weeks after the worst part of the cold is over.

☎ CALL YOUR PEDIATRICIAN IF

· a fever under 102°F lasts more than three days or fever over 102°F lasts more than twenty-four hours.

IS IT A COLD OR IS IT ALLERGY?

Allergies cause sneezing, nasal discharge, and coughing similar to a cold. Sometimes it is difficult to tell a cold from an allergy attack, especially because allergies can make children feel miserable and act sick while children with a cold often do not act very ill. Also, children may not show seasonal patterns to allergies the way adults do.

In general, however, a few features may help to distinguish colds from allergies:

▪ Colds may have a fever, allergies rarely do.

▪ Allergies cause itchy nose and throat, leading to nose twitching, throat clearing, and a characteristic "allergic salute," wiping the nose upward with the heel of the hand, even when it is not running.

▪ Colds produce thick, cloudy mucus, with inflamed and tender nasal membranes, while allergies cause thin, clear, watery nasal discharge.

- nasal discharge remains yellow and thick after the cold is over.
- nasal congestion prevents your infant from drinking.
- your baby is pulling at an ear or your older child complains of ear pain.
- the cold becomes progressively worse instead of better after one to three days.
- the cold lasts more than ten days. This could be a sign of a sinus infection.

B. Foul-Smelling Discharge from One Side of the Nose

When a bad smell and thick, yellow drainage come from one nostril, the chances are great that your child stuffed something up inside the nose that does not belong there. Children put the most outlandish things up their noses. I have removed nuts, foam rubber, beads, rocks, and candy. Doing that once is normal, but children who repeatedly insert foreign objects anywhere into their bodies—noses, ears, or vaginas—should be looked at carefully for psychological problems.

♥ IT IS NORMAL FOR

- children to put things into their noses. If you didn't see it go in, you will soon know by the smell and discharge.

☞ SEE YOUR PEDIATRICIAN IF

- you saw something go into a nostril but did not see it come out.
- you see something strange up your child's nostril.
- you notice drainage and/or a smell. Your pediatrician has special instruments to remove small objects from small noses.
- your child habitually inserts things where they shouldn't go.

C. Nosebleed

One of the reasons children have so many nosebleeds is that they spend so much time with their fingers in their noses. Other common causes are dry indoor air or an irritated nasal lining from a cold or allergy.

The sight of blood covering your child's face is a natural heart sinker for a parent but there usually is less blood than you think. A little blood can spread over a wide area. Simple measures usually stop the bleeding, but all sorts of folk remedies have developed over the centuries that do no good at all.

DO NOT
- put cold compresses or ice under the nose, in back of the head, or on the forehead.
- pack the nose with anything—it will not stop the bleeding and might well get stuck in there.
- panic if your child throws up blood. A lot of blood can be swallowed during a brisk nosebleed and blood in the stomach often causes vomiting.

DO
- have your child sit up and lean forward slightly so that blood does not go down the back of the throat.
- pinch the nostrils, holding the tip of the nose and pressing against the middle wall. Hold for at least ten minutes. Resist the urge to release the pressure every few seconds to see if the bleeding stopped.
- ask your pediatrician about using decongestant nasal drops for controlling nosebleeds.

♥ IT IS NORMAL FOR
- children to have occasional nosebleeds.
- children to vomit blood after a nosebleed.

☎ CALL YOUR PEDIATRICIAN IF
- the bleeding does not stop after twenty minutes of direct pressure.

- your child feels faint or dizzy *after* everyone else has calmed down.
- nosebleeds recur with any regularity or severity.
- there are any signs of other abnormal bleeding such as large, unexplained bruises or showers of tiny little red spots under the skin, which can be a sign of blood-clotting problems.

| 5 | NECK |

A. Swollen Glands

Lymph nodes or "glands" are infection-fighting organs located all over our bodies; we have them in the neck, under our arms, in the groin, and around the elbows, among other places. Because children have so many upper respiratory infections, the glands around the head and neck are constantly called upon to keep infections under control and make antibodies against invading germs. These glands are often working when your child has no evidence of having an infection.

Because of this, you are likely to see or feel glands from the size of a pea to that of a large walnut in the neck and the back of the head. Nearly half of all two-year-olds have some easily felt glands, and the percentage increases with increasing age of the child. Many skinny boys with long, thin necks have easily visible lymph nodes when they turn their head.

Some infections such as mononucleosis cause huge swollen glands.

As long as the glands move freely under your fingers and are firm but not rock hard or "stuck" together, their presence means only that your child has a healthy, working immune system.

♥ IT IS NORMAL FOR

- children to have glands in the neck that are easy to see or feel, with or without evidence of a current infection.

☎ CALL YOUR PEDIATRICIAN IF

- · the glands are extremely large, hard as a rock, clustered together in a large mass, or have overlying redness.
- · the glands are tender when you touch them.
- · they persist for more than three to four weeks.

B. Stiff Neck, Twisted Neck

The most serious problem associated with a stiff neck is meningitis, but fortunately it is the least likely. The stiff neck associated with meningitis involves stiffness of the muscles in the back of the neck and the upper back. The child cannot bend the head forward, and there is usually a severe headache, fever, and either irritability or extreme listlessness. An infant or toddler who is unable to tell you that her neck is sore will lie very still to avoid painful movement.

To test for stiffness associated with meningitis, you can ask an older child to put the chin down on the chest. Trying to flex the neck of a toddler almost always meets with resistance. It works better if you ask your toddler to look at his belly button or put something interesting in his lap.

The most common kind of stiff neck is the one that children wake up with after "sleeping wrong," or develop in association with a minor viral illness or sore lymph nodes (glands) in the neck. With that kind of stiff neck, children hold the head to one side and have difficulty moving it from side to side, but can usually bend the neck forward to touch the chin to the chest. Often it is difficult to bend the neck back to look upward. Although children will guard their necks from painful movement, they are able to walk and talk normally and do not look sick, and obviously do not have anything as serious as meningitis.

Sometimes a swollen, tender lymph node on one side of the neck from an infection can cause spasm of a neck muscle on that side.

Warm compresses and waiting a day for improvement is usually all that is necessary for a simple stiff neck. If pain is severe, symptoms persist several days, or the stiff neck developed after an accident or injury, see your pediatrician. A few sessions of physical therapy may relieve the pain of a simple stiff neck. Abnormalities of the vertebrae or smoldering infections may also be a cause.

♥ IT IS NORMAL FOR

· children to have a stiff neck with a minor illness or injury.

☎ CALL YOUR PEDIATRICIAN *IMMEDIATELY* IF

· a stiff neck is associated with fever, headache, or rash (especially one that looks like bruises).
· a stiff neck is associated with a bulging soft spot on the top of the head in an infant.
· symptoms of irritability, confusion, or poor coordination accompany a stiff neck.
· a stiff neck appeared after an injury.

☞ MAKE AN APPOINTMENT TO SEE YOUR PEDIATRICIAN IF

· your child has no other signs of illness but is holding the head to one side for more than a day.
· there are swollen glands or a tender muscle along with a twisted neck.

---

6 | MOUTH

A. Sores in the Mouth

Herpes virus causes cold sores on the outside edge of the lip and sometimes inside the mouth. Herpes infections of the mouth are usually accompanied by fever and swollen neck glands. Open ulcers on the gums, tongue, and palate and inside the lips take seven to fourteen days to heal but are painful for only five to seven days.

Canker sores are also found inside the lips and cheeks, but are particularly common where the gums meet the inside edge of the lip. Nobody knows what causes canker sores, although some people get them when they eat certain foods—nuts, tomatoes, and chocolate particularly.

Another cause of sores in the mouth is *hand, foot, mouth syndrome*. A viral infection that occurs in summer and early fall, it cause painless blisters on the palms and soles and painful ulcers in the mouth and on the inside of the lips.

The major problem with any sore mouth is that it may prevent your child from drinking enough fluids. Cool, bland foods such as Popsicles or Jell-O work better than acid liquids like fruit juices for a child with a sore mouth.

♥ IT IS NORMAL FOR
- children to have occasional canker sores in their mouths.
- herpes infections of the mouth to cause fever and swollen glands.

☎ CALL YOUR PEDIATRICIAN IF
- the pain is severe and you cannot relieve it with simple pain medication and icy foods such as Popsicles.
- your child refuses fluids and does not urinate for six to eight hours or more at a time.
- the canker sores last more than two weeks.
- a herpes infection is causing a high temperature and/or your child is acting very sick.
- your child is worse after a few days instead of better.

B. Tongue Tie

A little band of tissue connects the underneath side of the tongue with the floor of the mouth. This band, called the *lingual frenulum,* is shorter in some babies than in others. People used to think that if this band is too short, the tongue will not be able to move freely enough for clear speech.

Previous generations blithely cut this during the first year if the tongue seemed too tightly attached, under the mistaken notion that speech problems could thereby be avoided.

The truth is that an abnormally short frenulum is extremely rare, and only once in a great while is it necessary to cut into this tissue. In fact, after more than twenty years in practice I have seen only one child in whom this was necessary. There is always a risk of infection or bleeding not to mention pain with any incision, so there should be a darn good reason to invade your child's body this way.

♥ IT IS NORMAL FOR

• babies to have a tight attachment between the tongue and the floor of the mouth.

☎ CALL YOUR PEDIATRICIAN IF

• your relatives are giving you a hard time about it.

C. Irregular or Maplike Surface of the Tongue

The surface of the tongue is covered with small projections called *papillae* which function for our sense of taste. Sometimes areas of papillae become smooth and encircled by elevated gray margins, and the areas change from one day to the next. Known as *geographic tongue* because these areas look like continents on a map, this painless condition is seen in people with psoriasis, can be brought on by certain foods or mouthwashes, and sometimes appears with a viral infection. In the majority of cases, however, there is no ready explanation and it goes away on its own. There is no loss of taste.

♥ IT IS NORMAL FOR

- children to have a geographic tongue from time to time, sometimes lasting months to years.

D. Bad Breath

Sometimes I can tell from several feet away before I look at a child's throat that there is a strep infection, because strep imparts a particular odor to the breath. Children's breath often smells bad when they are sick because they are not eating and drinking enough to lubricate the mouth.

If bad breath is a persistent or recurring problem, it may come from poor dental hygiene or thumb sucking. For some reason a thumb and/or blanket in the mouth causes a bad odor, but this will disappear once the thumb sucking is given up.

A foreign object in the nose can cause what seems to be bad breath. When children slip something into their noses without parents knowing about it and the object stays there for any length of time, there is a distinctive, acrid odor that signals to pediatricians that there is something hiding up there.

If your child has bad breath, make certain it is coming from the mouth and not the nose.

♥ IT IS NORMAL FOR

- children to have occasional bad breath in the morning or when they are ill.
- children who suck their thumbs to have bad breath.

☎ CALL YOUR PEDIATRICIAN IF

- the odor seems to be coming from the nose. Bring your child in to have the object removed.
- the odor persists for no apparent reason.

E. Blue or Purple Bump on the Gum

When baby teeth come through the gums, some infants develop an ugly, reddish-blue bump on the gum which looks as though it hurts like crazy but it usually doesn't. Known as an *eruption cyst,* it will go away as soon as the tooth breaks through.

If the bump seems tender, you can do what you normally do for teething pain—apply teething gel, give your child a cold object such as a chilled teething ring to chew on, or give her a dose of acetaminophen (aspirin-free pain reliever).

♥ IT IS NORMAL FOR

• children to have ugly blue eruption cysts on their gums while they are teething.

F. White Patches in the Mouth

Flat, white patches that look like milk curds or cottage cheese on the inside of the cheeks, palate, gums, or tongue are caused by a fungus called monilia. Known as *thrush,* this infection is especially common in infants and toddlers who are breast or bottle feeding, but can also occur in older children after a course of antibiotics.

Sometimes babies also have a diaper rash from this same fungus after a course of antibiotics.

Mild cases clear up by themselves. If your doctor prescribes oral drops to treat the thrush, remember that the medicine works by being in contact with the membranes in the mouth, not by being absorbed through the stomach. Be sure to give the drops to your child after feeding and do not give water to wash it down. You want it to sit in the mouth for a while.

♥ IT IS NORMAL FOR

• children to develop a fungal infection of their mouth while nursing or after taking antibiotics. (Persistent fungal infections are accompanied by a hoarse voice; this can mean an infection lower down in the throat.)

☎ CALL YOUR PEDIATRICIAN IF

·   you notice a fungal infection. A course of oral drops usually clears it up.

·   your child has repeated bouts, or the thrush does not clear after one or two courses of medicine.

| 7 | THROAT |

A. Sore Throat; Sticking Fingers in the Mouth

Children who are too young to tell you their throat hurts may refuse to eat, stick their fingers deep into their mouths, or cry during feedings.

A sore throat without any accompanying symptoms such as a cold, fever, or cough may be due to dry air, tobacco smoke in the environment, or mouth breathing. A child who sleeps with an open mouth or one who is suffering because of dry air will usually get better after drinking some liquids.

A sore throat with a fever is most likely a viral infection which will last three or four days and get better on its own. However, about 10 percent of sore throats may be due to strep, a bacteria that can not only make children acutely ill but can, in rare instances, lead to complications such as rheumatic fever and kidney inflammation.

The only way to know for sure if a sore throat is due to strep is for your doctor to take a throat culture or do a rapid strep test.

Strep throat often causes swollen glands in the neck as well as fever and pain, but other infections can cause the same picture. Mononucleosis, for example, can resemble strep throat and is usually diagnosed by a blood test after the strep test is negative.

♥ IT IS NORMAL FOR

• children to have sore throats in the morning when the air is dry, such as when heat has been on overnight.

• children to have sore throats when exposed to tobacco smoke.

☞ MAKE AN APPOINTMENT WITH YOUR PEDIATRICIAN IF

• your child is mildly sick, in order to have a throat culture.

☎ CALL YOUR PEDIATRICIAN *IMMEDIATELY* IF

• your child cannot talk or swallow saliva. There may be a swelling in the throat which can obstruct breathing.

• your child has trouble opening the mouth. This can mean an abscess around the tonsils—more common in preteens and teens than in toddlers.

• breathing is noisy or difficult beyond just a stuffy nose.

• your child acts very sick.

B. Red Throat

Since most parents have never looked at their children's throats except when they are sick, they almost always think the throat is red. Unless you find pus covering the tonsils, a foul-smelling throat, or bright red spots on the palate as well as on the back of the throat, don't rely on your own diagnosis.

♥ IT IS NORMAL FOR

• a child's throat to seem red to parents looking at it with a flashlight in the middle of the night.

☎ CALL YOUR PEDIATRICIAN IF

• there is pus in the throat.

• the throat smells bad.

• there are swollen glands in the neck.

C. Spots on Tonsils

Tonsils are a kind of lymph node, the infection-fighting organs found in the neck and other places (see the section on swollen glands, page 66). You may see a lacy white covering on the tonsils from time to time, but if your child is not sick, there is no need to do anything about it.

When children reach the preteen years, tonsils start to shrink. During this time, they may develop pits which can hold debris from food and from the tissue being shed by the shrinking tonsils. When this debris collects over several weeks, it can become firm and yellow and resemble a kernel of corn. It will come out by itself eventually, and usually causes no discomfort.

♥ IT IS NORMAL FOR

- a bit of material to collect on the surface of children's tonsils from time to time.

☎ CALL YOUR PEDIATRICIAN IF

- there is dense, chalky white, or cottage cheese–like material covering the tonsils, especially if it extends to the palate or cheeks. This could be a fungal infection.
- your child is acting sick.
- there is a fever as well.

CHAPTER III

Air Passages, Lungs, & Chest

| 1 | COUGHING |

Coughing actually serves a purpose beyond annoying people and disturbing sleep. It is the way the lungs protect themselves from invasion by chemicals and germs and also a way to remove irritating material such as mucus and pus. Sometimes, however, coughs are stimulated by irritation of the lining membranes when there isn't really anything harmful there.

Wet coughs that bring up phlegm are no more or less serious than dry, unproductive coughs. What is more important is whether or not there is a fever as well, how long the cough lasts, whether it is getting better or worse, the age of the child, and what other symptoms (wheezing, vomiting, or abdominal pain, for example) go along with it.

Children may sound as though they are bringing something up when they cough, but they never spit it out. Adults can give their doctors a sputum specimen, but children, much to parents' and pediatricians' chagrin, swallow the stuff until they are well over age six.

A. Coughs in Infants

Coughs in the first few weeks are of more concern than they are later in life. Although small infants might have nothing more than the family cold, a cough that lasts more than a day or two, that interferes with feeding or is associated with even a slight fever should be checked out by your pediatrician. Small infants are more prone to pneumonia and other serious lung problems because their air tubes are so small and their cough is so weak that they cannot clear germs or mucus from their chests as well as older children.

Chlamydia is an infection that babies catch in the birth canal at the time of birth. It can cause a persistent, dry, sharp cough starting at six weeks which often does not make an infant severely ill at first. The possibility of chlamydia pneumonia is increased if your baby had a bout of conjunctivitis (pinkeye) during the first to second week of life. Chlamydia can be treated with an antibiotic.

Bronchiolitis is an infection caused by *respiratory syncytial virus* (RSV), to which infants are particularly susceptible. The major signs of bronchiolitis are rapid breathing along with a dry cough. A high-pitched, wheezing sound with breathing is also characteristic, but you may not be able to hear the wheezing without a stethoscope. The major sign of bronchiolitis is rapid, shallow breathing along with a dry cough. Sometimes the spaces between the ribs sink in when the baby takes a breath. Although there is no medication that will eliminate the virus, treatment with medications for asthma may relieve symptoms.

Children with bronchiolitis who are seriously ill may need to be hospitalized and treated with a special inhaled medication.

Whooping cough is fortunately still rare, but with the increasing number of unimmunized or inadequately immunized children in our country, the chances are increasing. Whooping cough is particularly serious in infants. Cold symptoms escalate into an increasingly severe cough with lots of clear, frothy mucus coming up through the nose and mouth. Characteristically, babies turn blue and make a whooping sound as the coughing spell ends.

Infants under two months, however, may have whooping cough with all the other symptoms but not make the whooping sound.

There is no cure for whooping cough and infants often need to be in the hospital until they are over the worst part. Whooping cough can be fatal or cause lasting brain or lung damage, so be sure your child has received all the required immunizations to prevent the disease.

On rare occasions a *persistent cough* in an infant is due to a malformation in the lung, the esophagus, or some other structure in the chest, or to a backup of stomach contents which irritates the lungs.

⊗ IT IS *NOT* NORMAL FOR

• infants to cough unless they have a cold, and then only for a few days.

☞ SEE YOUR PEDIATRICIAN IF

• *any cough lasts more than a day or two in a small infant,* especially if associated with a fever.

• coughing is severe enough to interfere with feeding or makes the baby gag and choke.

• your child's cough is accompanied by a lot of mucus from the nose and mouth with or without a whooping sound at the end.

• any cough is associated with a high fever.

B. Colds and Flu

With a simple cold or flu, a tight cough for the first few days accompanied by a runny or stuffy nose and other cold symptoms is followed by a looser cough which may persist on and off for as long as two weeks.

If it gradually decreases in frequency and severity, and your child appears well, wait it out.

If coughing persists two weeks after the onset of a cold and does not seem to be getting better, especially if there is some cloudy, green, or yellow nasal discharge or the cough is worse when your child lies down, it may have turned into a *sinus infection*. Sinus infections in children are different from those in adults. Grown-ups with sinus infections complain of facial pain and pressure or headache, and may have swollen eyes and tender cheeks. Children do not develop such specific symptoms. Sinus infections in children can be confirmed by an x-ray or ultrasound and may need more than one course of antibiotics before they clear up.

A child who suffers a prolonged cough after every cold may have a form of *asthma*. Although asthma is more likely in children with a history of allergies and hay fever, there may be no other sign but a tendency to cough with colds, when exposed to cold air, or with vigorous exercise. There are painless tests that can reveal the tendency to asthma in your child's lungs, and new treatments are effective with minimal side effects.

If your child has a severe or recurrent cough (especially if you remember an episode of choking in the recent past), there may be a *foreign body* in the lungs: peanuts, toy parts, coins, almost anything small enough may be inhaled. See "Chronic Cough," page 85.

♥ IT IS NORMAL FOR

· children to have a cough for two to four weeks after a cold or other respiratory infection.

☎ CALL YOUR PEDIATRICIAN IF

· the cough is not getting better or is getting worse.

· your child coughs after exercise or with exposure to cold air.

· your child has a prolonged cough along with and after most colds.

C. Bronchitis and Pneumonia

Bronchitis and pneumonia are infections that have extended lower down into the respiratory tract than a simple cold. In bronchitis, the infection is limited to the area in and around the air tubes, while pneumonia involves the lung tissue. Sometimes it is difficult for your pediatrician to draw the line; where does a bad case of bronchitis end and a mild case of pneumonia begin? Both of them make children cough, and may or may not cause a fever. X-rays are not always helpful, but actually it does not really matter because the treatment is similar for both.

Pneumonia and bronchitis can be caused by viruses or bacteria. Sometimes it is obvious that there is a bacterial infection, but most of the time it is difficult to tell the difference. Viral infections clear up by themselves, and bacterial infections may need the help of an antibiotic. Most pediatricians will treat bronchitis and pneumonia with antibiotics unless they are really sure the infections are caused by a virus.

Although it can become serious, pneumonia is not like pregnancy; you can have a little and get over it quickly.

It is *not* true that if you treat a cold right away you can keep a child from getting pneumonia. How I wish that were the case. We have also been led to believe that getting chilled can cause pneumonia—remember all the movies where people went out in the rain and five minutes later they were on their deathbeds coughing? That's not true either.

It is also not true that having a case of pneumonia "weakens the lungs" and makes a child more susceptible to it again. Children who have repeated episodes of pneumonia have an underlying reason that makes them more susceptible—asthma, for example, or living in a home with tobacco smoke. An otherwise healthy child can get over one bout of pneumonia without having to worry about another.

By the way, just to complicate the picture, it is possible for children to have pneumonia without coughing and with little or no abnormalities on physical examination. Sometimes only by taking an x-ray when your child has a mysterious fever can your pediatrician make the diagnosis.

♥ IT IS NORMAL FOR

• children to come down with pneumonia once or twice during childhood, especially if they are in group day-care, live in a home with tobacco smoke, or have asthma.

☞ SEE YOUR PEDIATRICIAN IF

• a cough associated with fever persists for more than a few days.
• your child appears sicker than you would expect with just a cold.

D. Laryngitis, Hoarseness, Loss of Voice

Laryngitis usually starts suddenly—your child wakes up in the morning without a voice. There may have been a mild cold for a day or two before, but often there is no preceding infection. Sometimes children with laryngitis wake up in the middle of the night with a high-pitched cough similar to croup, and then the cough is gone by morning along with the voice.

The cause of laryngitis is almost always a viral infection with little or no fever, and your child's voice should return in a day or two. Sometimes older children who were yelling at an athletic event will lose their voice the next day because their vocal cords are irritated by overuse. This will also get better in a day or two. Enjoy the silence while it lasts.

If your hoarse child is having trouble breathing or swallowing, go to your pediatrician's office or an emergency room immediately. These are signs that there may be a dangerous swelling in the throat that can obstruct the airway. If your child has a high fever, severe throat pain, or the hoarseness lasts more than three to five days, see your pediatrician.

An infant with an unusually deep, hoarse voice may have growths in the throat called *laryngeal papillomas.* These growths do not cause any distress or respiratory problems until they grow large enough to obstruct the airway, so it is important to diagnose them before that happens. If your baby has an unusually deep, "sexy" voice, bring it to your pediatrician's attention.

☆ IT IS COMMON FOR
· children to suffer a sudden loss of voice for a day or two.

☞ SEE YOUR PEDIATRICIAN *IMMEDIATELY* IF
· your child has a high fever, or difficulty breathing or swallowing along with loss of voice or hoarseness.

☞ MAKE AN APPOINTMENT WITH YOUR PEDIATRICIAN IF
· hoarseness persists for more than two to three days.
· your child develops an unusually deep voice.

E. Sudden, "Barking" Cough; Croup

Croup is frightening for many reasons, not least of which is that it often starts suddenly in the middle of the night—a time when everything is scarier. Your child may or may not have had cold symptoms prior to the onset of a barking, seal-like cough and, sometimes, a high-pitched, crowing sound when your child inhales. The more upset your child becomes, the worse the barking cough becomes. In turn, the more difficult it becomes to move air in and out, and completing the circle, the more frightened your child becomes.

The fever that often accompanies croup can also

make it worse; the higher the fever, the faster a child breathes, which makes the coughing worse.

There are some measures you can take to relieve your child's distress temporarily. Steam up the bathroom by running the hot water in the shower with the doors and windows closed, sit in there for a few minutes, and try to calm your child. In a little while the hot steam and reassurance almost always make breathing easier. Set up a humidifier in your child's bedroom to continue the humidity and set up a cot or sleeping bag for yourself in your child's room so you can monitor breathing through the night.

If your child continues to make a "crowing" sound when breathing in even after calming down, if you cannot make your child comfortable, or if your child seems to be having serious trouble breathing (spaces between the ribs sink in with each breath, unable to lie down) or has poor color—gray, blue, or pale—go to an emergency room at once. There is treatment available with inhaled medication that can open up the air passages.

♥ IT IS NORMAL FOR
- children to develop croup suddenly in the middle of the night.

☎ CALL YOUR PEDIATRICIAN *IMMEDIATELY* OR GO TO AN EMERGENCY ROOM IF
- your child cannot swallow liquids or is drooling and reluctant to swallow saliva.
- your child cannot talk.
- your child has poor color—gray, blue, pale.
- your child is agitated and cannot be calmed down (this can be a sign that not enough air is getting through).
- your child is breathing more easily and is settled down but makes a "crowing" sound when taking in a breath.
- breathing seems to take a great deal of effort.

F. Chronic Cough

Chronic coughs are ones that persist longer than four weeks. The most common reason for a chronic cough is *cough variant asthma*. This type of cough is made worse by exercise, a cold, or exposure to cold air, dust, pollen, or animals. It is a form of allergic asthma. Children with cough variant asthma may have a history of hay fever symptoms, eczema, or allergies, or have a family history of allergies or asthma.

> ⊗ Children who live with *tobacco smoke* have more frequent, more severe, and more prolonged respiratory problems than children who live in smoke-free environments, so a simple cough can hang on for extra weeks because of tobacco smoke. If you smoke and you are not ready to stop, confine your smoking to areas where your children are not present and do not ever smoke in the car when your children are along, even with the windows open. Make sure there is no smoke at day-care, also.

Children who have a persistent cough with or without a runny nose for ten to thirty days after a cold, with little or no fever and sometimes foul-smelling breath, may have a *sinus infection*. In adults, sinus infections often cause facial pain, swollen eyes, or headache, but children have less specific symptoms. Your pediatrician may need to take an x-ray or order an ultrasound to diagnose it.

Infection with a germ called *mycoplasma* can cause fever and coughing, and the cough can persist for as long as one to three months after the fever subsides. This is diagnosed with a blood test and can be cured with erythromycin, an antibiotic.

I once entered an examination room and found the mother of a patient waiting for me alone. When I asked her what was wrong, she burst into tears and said, "Why didn't you tell me he had *cystic fibrosis?*"

She had read the report of his chest x-ray at the last visit when he had bronchitis and put together the fact that he was a skinny child and had frequent coughs and convinced herself that he had CF. Actually, he turned out to have allergies.

Cystic fibrosis can cause a chronic cough, but there are usually other symptoms such as poor weight gain, large greasy stools, wheezing, and pneumonias. Children with long-term or recurrent cough are often tested for cystic fibrosis, even when a pediatrician thinks it is unlikely. The test is painless and the disease should be ruled out.

Other causes for a chronic cough include a *foreign body in the lung* (often a peanut, but just about anything that is small enough for a child to inhale), an undiagnosed *infection* such as *tuberculosis* or a *fungus infection,* or a congenital *malformation* involving the lung.

♥ IT IS NORMAL FOR

• children to have a lingering cough for several weeks after a cold.

☎ CALL YOUR PEDIATRICIAN IF

• the cough following a cold is not improving after two weeks.

• your child coughs after exercise or after exposure to cold air, dust, or other irritants.

• you need a referral to a smoking cessation program.

---

2 | BREATHING PROBLEMS

A. Trouble Breathing

When I was first in practice and my answering service would say, "Mrs. Jones is on the phone. Her daughter Allison can't breathe," my heart would squeeze and I would go through a mental checklist for what to do about respiratory failure while waiting to be connected.

I soon learned that "can't breathe" usually means a stuffy nose.

Newborns are notorious for having a whole symphony of nasal noises because they cannot sniffle or blow the mucus out of their noses. Snorting, sniffing, mouth breathing, or chest rattling in a child who can drink, talk, and play does not really mean that breathing is difficult, only noisy (see C., "Noisy Breathing," below). What I am talking about here is serious trouble moving air in and out of the lungs.

Difficulty getting air *into* the lungs can come from a swelling of the epiglottis, the flap in the throat that closes off the airway when you swallow, from an object stuck in the throat, or from swelling of the lining of the throat in croup or other respiratory infections. Children with obstructed intake often make a crowing noise when breathing in.

Difficulty getting air *out* of the lungs occurs with bronchiolitis asthma, (see pages 78, 80), or some other infection that swells the lining of the air tubes, or a foreign body or growth in the airway.

♥ IT IS NORMAL FOR
   · children to have noisy breathing with a cold.
   · you to be able to feel a rattle or vibration in the chest when childen have mucus in their air passages.

☎ CALL YOUR PEDIATRICIAN IF
   · your child is not seriously ill but you can hear a wheeze.

☞ SEE YOUR PEDIATRICIAN OR GO TO AN EMERGENCY ROOM
   IMMEDIATELY IF
   · breathing trouble has developed suddenly.
   · breathing is very rapid or very labored.

- there are abnormal sounds along with breathing—grunting, crowing, whistling, a moan, a groan, or an "uh" sound with each breath.
- there is sinking in of the spaces between the ribs or where the ribs meet the abdomen with each breath.
- your child has difficulty getting a breath in.
- breathing trouble is associated with anxiety, drooling, inability to talk or swallow, and/or poor color.

A GRUNTING SOUND

A MOAN, GROAN, OR "UH" WHEN BREATHING OUT—SHOULD ALWAYS BE CONSIDERED A SIGN OF SERIOUS TROUBLE. Severe asthma, shock from an overwhelming infection, heart failure, and a host of other serious problems may cause grunting. If you notice it even slightly, go to your pediatrician or an emergency room immediately.

Also, if your child makes no noise at all, drools because it is difficult to swallow saliva, does not want to speak, and sits upright with the head forward or is extremely pale, gray, or bluish, get your child to an emergency room immediately.

B. Breathing Too Fast

The normal rate of breathing decreases from forty breaths per minute at birth to twenty breaths per minute, the normal rate for adults, by adolescence. Children breathe more rapidly when they have a fever, when you can feel the heart beating rapidly and strongly as well. If you notice your feverish child is breathing rapidly, bring the fever down to see if the breathing rate falls also, before you worry.

Some medications such as asthma medicines and cold preparations can speed up the pulse and respiratory rate.

A newborn or infant under three months may

breathe rapidly merely because her nose is plugged up from a cold. At this age, babies can only breathe through their noses, not their mouths, except when they cry, so when they are not crying, they need to breathe more rapidly and shallowly to get enough air in and out. When they cry, however, they take air in through their mouths and have no trouble breathing at all.

Children with an asthma attack may breathe quickly even without any audible wheezing. Babies with bronchiolitis (see page 78), a viral infection that causes the airways to narrow, may breathe rapidly with or without a dry cough.

Some serious problems such as heart failure and dangerous infections can also raise breathing rate.

♥ IT IS NORMAL FOR
   · children to breathe at a rate of forty breaths per minute in early infancy, thirty per minute when toddlers, and twenty per minute by adolescence.
   · children with fevers to breathe more rapidly.

☎ CALL YOUR PEDIATRICIAN IF
   · breathing is more rapid than forty in an infant, or thirty to thirty-five in a child over two with no discernible cause such as a fever.

☞ SEE YOUR PEDIATRICIAN OR GO TO AN EMERGENCY ROOM IF
   · rapid breathing is associated with grunting, poor color, or anxiety.
   · a moan, groan, or "uh" sound accompanies each breath.
   · your child is making wheezing, crowing, or whistling sounds.

C. Noisy Breathing

Even a small amount of mucus in the tiny air passages of an infant can set up quite a din. Snorting and gurgling sounds coming from an otherwise comfortable baby who is able to nurse or bottle-feed and sleep without any problem is normal.

When your baby has a cold, a bit of mucus trapped in the throat or windpipe may cause a vibration that you can feel with your hand on your baby's chest. It is there because your baby does not know how to go "harumph" and clear the throat yet. Usually this goes away with a good cough, returning when mucus collects again. This does not mean that your child has pneumonia.

Healthy infants who have constant noisy breathing from birth or shortly thereafter might have a weakness or softness of the cartilage of the larynx (voice box), or the trachea. This condition goes away gradually as the tissue hardens in the first year of life.

Noises like crowing, barking, wheezing, grunting, or whistling along with a fever in a child who looks or acts unwell may indicate some problem moving air in and out of the lungs. It could be a swelling in the throat or lungs, a foreign object, or an abnormal growth (see A., "Trouble Breathing," above).

Noisy breathing when children sleep can be caused by large adenoids or chronic nasal congestion from allergies. If there are pauses of several seconds between breaths while your child is sleeping, the problem may be *sleep apnea*. This disturbance of normal sleep patterns can lead to other medical problems if it is not treated.

♥ IT IS NORMAL FOR

• infants and small children to make all sorts of strange noises when they have mucus in their air passages.

• you to feel a vibration on your child's chest when mucus causes noisy breathing.

☞ SEE YOUR PEDIATRICIAN IF

• there is any difficulty with breathing, inability to feed, a crowing or barking sound, wheezing, or poor color.

· your child appears anxious or frightened, which may be a sign that not enough oxygen is getting in.

· noisy breathing is accompanied by any other signs of illness.

· your child wakes from sleep because of noisy, obstructed breathing or has long pauses between noisy breaths while sleeping.

D. Wheezing

A wheeze is a high-pitched, almost musical sound made when air goes in or out of the lungs. Your pediatrician may hear it with a stethoscope and tell you it is there, but sometimes you can hear it with a naked ear.

The causes of wheezing are different for infants than they are for older children.

i. In Infants

A weakness or softness of the cartilage that supports the trachea can cause wheezing at or shortly after birth that is most pronounced when your baby exhales. If this wheezing does not interfere with feeding, and your baby is gaining weight and breathing comfortably, your pediatrician may do nothing about it except wait until the tissue hardens by itself.

Babies who were premature and needed oxygen and a machine to help their breathing at birth may develop scarring of the lungs called *bronchopulmonary dysplasia* (BPD). These babies start wheezing during infancy but usually not until after they have left the hospital. The disease looks, acts, and sounds like asthma and is treated similarly.

A virus called respiratory syncytial virus (RSV) causes a lung infection called *bronchiolitis,* to which children under two are particularly susceptible. Starting like a cold, in one or two days the infant starts to breathe rapidly and wheeze. Along with a dry cough, the area just under the rib cage and the spaces between the ribs may sink in with each breath, and the child's nostrils may flare as well. There may or may not be a fever. Infants with bronchiolitis can be mildly to seriously ill, and should be followed closely by their pediatrician through the often weeks-long course of the illness.

Sometimes a chemical or irritant in an infant's room can cause wheezing. When I was in medical school, I cared for a baby whose wheezing always cleared up in the hospital but who got deathly sick whenever he went home. It turned out he was reacting to baby powder, which the hospital never used. A colleague of mine took care of an infant with chronic wheezing problems which cleared up after his mother stopped spraying his nursery with a disinfectant. What she thought would keep him from getting sick was actually *making* him sick.

☆ IT IS COMMON BUT *NOT* NORMAL FOR
- infants to wheeze.

☞ SEE YOUR PEDIATRICIAN IF
- there is any episode of wheezing in an infant.
- recurrent episodes of wheezing come and go.
- there is wheezing in your infant who was premature and needed special care in the nursery.

☞ SEE YOUR PEDIATRICIAN *IMMEDIATELY* IF
- wheezing is severe.
- fever, poor color, or inability to feed accompanies wheezing.
- breathing is faster than forty breaths per minute.
- there is grunting (an "uh" sound or moan) with each breath.

ii. In Older Children

Some cold viruses and other respiratory infections can make children wheeze during the worst part of the cold.

If, however, your child wheezes repeatedly with infections or with exposure to cats, cold air, pollen, pollution, or other irritants, you may be dealing with asthma. The likelihood of asthma is increased if there is a history of allergies or asthma on either side of the family.

A child who wheezes, coughs, and is short of breath fifteen minutes after beginning exercise or four to twelve minutes after stopping may have *exercise-induced asthma*. This can occur in children who already have allergic asthma, but may strike children with no previous signs of respiratory problems.

Wheezing may accompany *cystic fibrosis* (CF), an inherited disease of the lungs and digestive tract. Children with CF are usually but not always small for their age or have poor weight gain. Small children with chronic wheezing should be tested for cystic fibrosis.

Sudden onset of wheezing may be a sign that your child inhaled an object into the airway. Pieces of hot dog, peanuts, candy, or small toy parts are the most common, but one of my patients managed to slip an antique Yugoslavian coin into his lung. Although most objects cause a constant wheeze, peanuts are notorious for causing intermittent wheezing that resembles asthma.

☆ IT IS COMMON FOR

· children to wheeze with some respiratory infections.

☞ SEE YOUR PEDIATRICIAN IF

· wheezing is recurrent.

· wheezing begins after a choking or vomiting episode.

· wheezing is associated with difficult breathing, poor color, and/or vomiting.

3	THE CHEST

A. Chest Pain

Chest pain in children, in contrast to adults, is rarely caused by heart problems. Most often the pain comes from irritation of muscles or cartilage around the ribs due to a viral infection. This type of pain comes and goes in twinges or causes a dull ache that grows worse with a deep breath. You can induce the same pain by pressing on or between the ribs.

Children with asthma who have been wheezing and coughing forcefully and repeatedly may develop pain due to sore chest muscles.

Pneumonia can cause chest pain, but usually there is also a fever and/or cough.

Sudden, severe chest pain can result from rupture of an air sac in the lung. Pain is produced when air leaks into the space between the lung and the chest wall. Called a pneumothorax, this can happen without any apparent cause, or can occur with asthma, pneumonia, or an injury to the chest.

Some older children suffer from *precordial catch syndrome*. While sitting quietly in school or at home, a sudden, sharp chest pain may be severe enough to make a child pale and frightened. The pain goes away in a few seconds to a minute or two. It is important that this pain is *not* related to exertion. Pain with exertion may signal a serious problem.

In rare instances, chest pain in children can be serious, if it is accompanied by nausea or vomiting, paleness, faintness, extreme fatigue, or poor color. Children who have had Kawasaki's disease, for example, (see page 173) are at risk for developing aneurysms (outpouchings) of the blood vessels of the heart which can cause heart attacks. Fever, rash, red eyes, cracked, crusted lips, and peeling fingers and toes a few weeks before the chest pain may indicate a serious problem.

Viral infections of the heart muscle *(myocarditis)* or, more commonly, infections of the covering around the heart *(pericarditis)* can cause chest pain which is severe and constant. Children with heart inflammation may sit upright and bend forward to relieve the pain. Rheumatic fever, while still uncommon, is on the rise and can also cause an inflammation of the heart. Usually children with rheumatic fever have some other signs of illness such as joint pain, a rash, a history of a sore throat, or fever.

Chest pain associated with any signs of illness should be evaluated and treated promptly.

♥ IT IS NORMAL FOR

· children to have occasional twinges of chest pain, especially with viral infections or after bouts of coughing.

☞ SEE YOUR PEDIATRICIAN IF

· chest pain is severe or unremitting.
· chest pain is associated with exertion.
· chest pain is associated with difficult breathing, poor color, fever, nausea, or vomiting or other signs of illness.

B. Sunken Chest

It is normal for infants to have a slight indentation at the bottom end of the breastbone and for that bone to sink in a little when they breathe, especially while crying vigorously.

In a few children, the indentation of the breastbone between the nipples becomes more and more pronounced over the years until they have an obviously sunken chest.

Although it looks as though this sunken chest should restrict a child's breathing and impair endurance, the truth is that only rarely is there a measurable effect on a child's stamina. More often the problem is that some children—boys particularly—are embarrassed by the way it looks. A boy who always swims with a shirt on, for example, may be having serious psychological effects from his sunken chest.

The ideal time for surgical repair of this *pectus excavatum*—whether for cosmetic or functional reasons—is between eight and nine years, when a child is large enough but the skeleton has not fully matured.

♥ IT IS NORMAL FOR
· some children to have a sunken chest.

☞ SEE YOUR PEDIATRICIAN IF
· you feel this is affecting your child's stamina.
· your child is embarrassed by the appearance of a sunken chest.

C. Breast Lumps

i. In Girls

Although the average age is eleven, some girls develop breast tissue as early as age eight. It starts as a painless or slightly tender, firm lump under one swollen nipple. The skin overlying it should not be red and there should be no discharge from the nipple. Although it is perplexing and sometimes worrisome to parents when this happens on one side only, within one to four months the other breast will usually start developing, and it then becomes clear this is not a tumor.

If this process starts before age 7½, it is called *premature thelarche,* or abnormally early breast development. If there are no other signs of puberty such as armpit or pubic hair, increased vaginal secretions, or a growth spurt, your doctor will probably recommend no further tests. If there are signs of early puberty, tests for hormone functions will have to be done.

♥ IT IS NORMAL FOR
· girls to start developing breast tissue as early as eight years.

☞ SEE YOUR PEDIATRICIAN IF
- breast tissue grows before age 7½.
- there is any secretion from the nipple.
- the skin surrounding the nipple is red.

ii. In Boys

Approximately 60–70 percent of males will develop some breast tissue early in the course of puberty. A nubbin of tissue under the nipple may be tender, and the nipple on one or both sides is raised and swollen. The vast majority of the time, this tissue disappears over one to two years.

If this tissue persists longer than two years, and especially if it is cosmetically annoying to your son, it can be removed.

♥ IT IS NORMAL FOR
- males to develop a little breast tissue early in puberty.

☞ SEE YOUR PEDIATRICIAN IF
- there is any discharge from the nipple.
- the swelling persists more than two years.
- breast tissue develops in your son long before there are any other changes of puberty.

D. Protruding Bony Lump at the Bottom of the Breastbone

The end of the breastbone (sternum) is formed by a small bone called the xiphoid process, which is triangular and sometimes loosely attached at the bottom point. It is not unusual for this bone to protrude or to be easily felt through the thin skin of a child's chest.

This is not a tumor or an abnormal growth, and you do not need to do anything about it.

♥ IT IS NORMAL FOR
- the tip of the breastbone to be easily seen or felt.

E. Chest Injuries

A blow to the chest from a baseball or falling onto a hard object can be more serious in a child than an adult. Children's ribs are softer and more pliable, and while that means that they have fewer rib fractures than adults, it also means that the ribs provide less protection to the heart and lungs from the force of an injury.

Therefore, if your child receives a chest injury severe enough to "knock the air out of him," see your pediatrician or go to an emergency room. Also, bleeding and bruising of the lungs or heart may not cause symptoms until some time after the injury, so any chest symptoms that develop in the following hours or days should be checked out.

☆ IT IS COMMON FOR

- children to receive injuries to the chest.

☞ SEE YOUR PEDIATRICIAN IF

- a chest injury is severe, even if your child seems all right.
- any symptoms of pain or breathing problems appear after a chest injury.

CHAPTER IV

Stomach, Bowels, & Abdomen

| 1 | SUDDEN ABDOMINAL PAIN |

When your child complains of stomach pain, chances are it is a minor problem. If vomiting and diarrhea follow shortly, it is probably due to a stomach flu that will resolve itself in a day or two. If your child ate something that did not agree with him, symptoms should be better in a few hours.

The chance that there is a serious problem increases if the pain grows steadily worse and your child looks sicker and sicker over the next few hours. Although appendicitis or a bowel obstruction can begin with a simple bellyache, sometimes abdominal pain is due to something that has nothing to do with the stomach or bowels—pneumonia in a lower lobe of the lung, a urinary tract infection, or even a strep throat.

Most children will point to their belly button when you ask where it hurts, so the location of the pain is rarely a useful piece of information.

A blow to the abdomen can cause abdominal pain

several days later. If a lap belt crosses the soft part of your child's abdomen instead of being supported by the pelvic bones as it is in adults, for example, and squeezes your child's belly during an accident, the intestinal walls may slowly swell and cause a bowel obstruction.

If you think your child's abdominal pain is from simple constipation, avoid giving your child any laxatives, enemas, or cramp medicine until you have waited two or three hours to see what happens. In most cases, the pain will go away or lessen by then, but if there is a serious problem, you could make things worse with these measures.

☎ CALL THE DOCTOR *IMMEDIATELY* OR GO TO AN EMERGENCY ROOM IF

   · crampy pain becomes constant.
   · constant pain persists more than two to three hours.
   · the pain is severe and unrelenting.
   · nausea and vomiting progress to constant vomiting (dry heaves) even without eating or drinking.
   · vomited material is brown or green.
   · your child refuses to walk or walks bent over.
   · pain extends to the scrotum or testicles.
   · there was a recent injury to the abdomen.
   · pain is accompanied by blood in the stool.
   · it hurts when you press on your child's belly.
   · the abdomen appears swollen or feels hard.
   · your child is acting very sick.

| 2 | CHRONIC OR RECURRENT ABDOMINAL PAIN |

The most common cause of long-standing abdominal pain in children is known as *recurrent abdominal pain of childhood* (RAP). This, of course, does not describe it; it merely names it.

RAP affects 12 to 15 percent of school-aged children and is not seen in children under three. It is characterized by bouts of abdominal pain that recur for three or more months, interfere with school and play, but seldom awaken children at night. The pain is particularly problematic at meal times, especially breakfast.

RAP is probably due to an inherited tendency toward stronger than normal bowel activity which causes cramping and pain. There is often a history of ulcers, colitis, or other stomach problems in the family. Constipation can accompany RAP, but is not a cause of it.

Although symptoms may become more severe or more frequent during times of stress, it is not purely a psychological problem.

If your pediatrician suspects RAP, the chances that your child has some serious underlying condition are slim—far less than 1 in 10. Nevertheless, children with RAP can get appendicitis or other serious problems just like other children. Call your pediatrician if there is a change in the character, severity, or pattern of the chronic pain.

Sensitivity to food can cause recurrent pain, especially sorbitol (the artificial sweetener in sugarless gum and other processed food), milk, or wheat. In these cases, however, there are usually other symptoms such as bloating, excessive gas, or diarrhea. Severe reactions to foods are often accompanied by signs of blood in the stool—either bright red or a black, tarlike color.

Rarely, colitis and other serious bowel problems cause chronic pain, but there are usually other symptoms such as fever, pain that wakens the child at night, weight loss, or slowing of growth.

☎ CALL YOUR DOCTOR IF YOUR CHILD HAS CHRONIC PAIN AND
- the pattern varies, that is, it becomes more severe or lasts longer than usual.
- the pain wakens your child at night.
- there is persistent or recurrent vomiting.

- there is crampy or bloody diarrhea.
- his stools are black as tar.
- there is weight loss or a slowing of growth in height.
- your child is awakened at night by the urge to have a bowel movement.
- there is joint pain or stiffness along with abdominal pain.
- there is bloating of the abdomen or visible bulges that move slowly across the abdomen when your child lies quietly.

---

3 | CONSTIPATION

Hundreds of millions of dollars are spent every year in this country on laxatives. Laxative manufacturers have done a great job of convincing Americans that we must have a bowel movement every day. That is simply not true, especially for children.

Constipation means the infrequent and difficult passage of hard, dry, painful stools. If your child has one soft bowel movement every few days but is comfortable in between, your child is not constipated. Daily "regularity" does not necessarily mean your child is healthier than a child who passes bowel movements at irregular intervals. Frequent (four times a day) or infrequent (once a week) bowel movements may be normal. It is not true that retained stool "poisons the system" or damages the intestine.

Constipation is common during the second year of life because of dietary changes, especially when cow's milk replaces formula or breast milk. Also, when toilet training starts and children learn to withhold stool, constipation may follow.

Other causes for occasional, minor constipation are:
- iron-containing medicine, antacids, or some other medications.

- illness with fever or vomiting causing decreased fluid intake.
- a diet low in fiber.

Many breastfed infants have infrequent stools and may even strain when passing stool, but bowel movements should be watery or loose. If yor baby consumes only breast milk and has hard stools, see your pediatrician.

Formula-fed infants may be constipated by a particular brand of formula. In that case, changing to another formula usually solves the problem.

Infants under age one who are constipated, are excessively tired, have a weak cry, feed poorly, are limp, and move less than normal may have *infant botulism*. Classical, adult-type botulism is caused by ingesting botulism toxin produced by a fungus that multiplies in improperly canned or preserved food. Infant botulism, on the other hand, happens when babies ingest the botulism spores themselves, which older children and adults can inactivate in their stomachs. Because babies have insufficient stomach acid to kill these spores, poison is produced in the intestine and absorbed as the spores pass through.

Honey is the major source for infant botulism. Avoid giving your baby any form of honey until the one year mark is passed.

Infants with persistent constipation from birth or shortly after must be checked for *Hirschsprung's disease,* a malfunction of a short segment of bowel which traps stool, prevents defecation, and can cause abdominal bloating and potentially serious illness if not diagnosed and treated.

Thyroid disorders and other hormone problems may also cause constipation.

Constipation can lead to an anal fissure—an irritation or cracking of the sensitive skin around the anus, which is prone to bleed, producing bright red blood on the outside of the stool.

Passing a painful stool may frighten your child into

holding back the urge to defecate. This results in the gradual accumulation of a large, hard mass of stool near the rectal opening. As your child withholds more and more, crankiness, reluctance to eat, overflow soiling in which loose stool leaks around the hard, impacted stool, and increasing fear of toileting create a vicious circle.

You can solve or prevent this problem by offering high-fiber foods and mild stool softeners or lubricants such as mineral oil by mouth to soften stool. The goal is to make having a bowel movement comfortable rather than painful and frightening. Suppositories and enemas may be helpful to clean out old, hard stool, but avoid them if your child is reluctant or fearful. Ask your pediatrician for a stool-softening regimen.

☎ CALL YOUR PEDIATRICIAN IF

• your child is otherwise well but constipation began shortly after introducing cow's milk, following an illness, or after a medication was begun.

• your child is otherwise well but you think there may not be enough fiber in the diet your child is eating.

☞ SEE YOUR PEDIATRICIAN IF

• your infant is constipated.

• your breastfed infant has hard stools.

• there is hard swelling of the abdomen associated with constipation.

• constipation is associated with vomiting, poor feeding, tiredness, or limpness.

• there is blood with the stool.

• your child is not gaining weight and developing normally.

| 4 | DIARRHEA |

Diarrhea means the passage of large, watery, and abnormally frequent stools. Breastfed babies may have six to ten small, watery stools per day, but that is not diarrhea if it is their normal pattern. Some children have looser than normal stools when they are teething or after they eat a particular food, but that usually clears up in less than twenty-four hours.

The loss of large amounts of body fluids with severe diarrhea can cause dehydration, and the risk is increased if your child is also vomiting. Dehydration from diarrhea causes the death of millions of children in the third world, but even in the United States, five hundred children die of this every year.

The most common cause of severe diarrhea in children is a virus called *rotavirus*. The risk of rotavirus infection is greatest from October through May but the illness occurs at other times of the year as well. It is common in infants and toddlers in day-care, but also occurs in children who are home with their mother all day.

Until recently, pediatricians advised parents to treat diarrhea with clear liquids followed by a restricted, constipating diet. Current studies have shown that not only is this not necessary, but it may actually prolong illness and even cause malnutrition if continued for too long.

Diarrhea accompanied by high fever, blood, or mucus in the stool and significant abdominal pain may be caused by a bacterial infection. Your pediatrician may order a stool culture and antibiotic treatment.

Large, frothy stools accompanied by stomach bloating and gas and a pattern that comes and goes over several weeks without making your child terribly sick may be caused by *giardia*. Previously, this microscopic parasite mainly infected hikers and campers who drank water from polluted streams but it has become common among urban and suburban children over the past ten years.

About 15 percent of healthy, active babies and toddlers start to pass loose stools and may do so for weeks or months at a time without becoming ill. Other than suffering a persistent diaper rash, these babies grow and develop normally. The stools may be watery or look like mucus, and contain visible remnants of fruits and vegetables your child ate.

Eliminating certain foods from the diet or diluting your baby's formula has little or no effect on this diarrhea pattern. Antidiarrhea medications seldom work and should not be used over long periods of time. The tendency for loose stools disappears before or by the third birthday in most cases. This kind of diarrhea is harmless.

☎ CALL YOUR PEDIATRICIAN IF

• you want instructions on how to treat your child's diarrhea if it continues for more than twenty-four to forty-eight hours without abating.

• your child is vomiting along with the diarrhea.

☞ SEE YOUR PEDIATRICIAN IF

• there is blood or mucus in the stool.

• your child has fever and/or severe abdominal pain.

• diarrhea is mild but continues for more than two weeks; is associated with bloating, gas, and frothy stools; or your child is losing weight.

☞ GO TO AN EMERGENCY ROOM OR YOUR PEDIATRICIAN'S OFFICE *IMMEDIATELY* IF

• your child has any of these signs of dehydration:
• sunken eyes
• a dry mouth
• does not cry tears
• does not urinate for six to eight hours
• poor color or doughy skin
• excessive listlessness or tiredness

5 | ABNORMAL STOOLS

A. Blood

Blood in the stool is always a cause for concern, but a small amount of bright red blood on the outside of a hard, constipated stool may be due to nothing more than a small tear of the skin around the anus, called an *anal fissure.* Painless bleeding in a child over the age of one year can also be due to polyps in the intestine or a malformation called *Meckel's diverticulum,* and children of any age can develop bleeding ulcers.

Some bowel infections can cause bleeding that may or may not be associated with fever, abdominal pain, or diarrhea.

A blob of bright red blood that looks like currant jelly may come from a kink in the bowel called an *intussuception.* This must be treated promptly because of the danger of bleeding and intestinal obstruction.

☞ **SEE YOUR PEDIATRICIAN IF**

• a small amount of bright red blood appears occasionally on the stool.

☞ **SEE YOUR PEDIATRICIAN OR GO TO AN EMERGENCY ROOM *IMMEDIATELY* IF**

• there is a large amount of blood on the stool or blood that looks like currant jelly.

• your child is also vomiting; has a bloated, tender, or hard abdomen; or is acting sick.

B. Red—Not Blood

Some medications and some processed foods that contain red dye may color your child's stool red, especially if your child is having diarrhea. Examples are red gelatin, fruit punch or Kool-Aid, tomato soup, beets, red licorice, liquid medications or vitamins with red dye, or laxatives (such as Ex Lax) that contain phe-nolphthalein.

♥ IT IS NORMAL FOR

· children to have red stools with certain foods or medicines.

☎ CALL YOUR PEDIATRICIAN IF

· you cannot figure out what caused the redness of the stool or the redness does not go away.

C. Black

The most worrisome cause for black stool is blood that has passed through the gastrointestinal tract and become partially digested. Stools that are black with blood will have a tarlike look. Other causes for black stool are:

· medications which contain iron
· medicines with bismuth, such as Pepto Bismol
· foods such as spinach, grape juice, or licorice
· eating material that contains lead such as old, peeling paint
· eating charcoal, coal, or dirt

♥ IT IS NORMAL FOR

· children to have black stools after eating certain foods or medication.

☞ SEE YOUR PEDIATRICIAN IF

· your child has been chewing on chipped paint or eats coal, soil, or charcoal habitually. (Craving for soil or other peculiar substances may signal anemia or other medical problems.)

☞ SEE YOUR PEDIATRICIAN *IMMEDIATELY* IF

· there is no obvious cause for black stool.
· black stools are associated with abdominal pain, paleness, or any other signs of illness.

D. Gritty

When your infant starts eating solid foods, bowel movements can go through all sorts of peculiar changes. Pears and some other fruits can cause a gritty texture as though tiny stones are mixed with stool. There is no harm in this, and no need to discontinue the fruit.

Toddlers and older children who have gritty stools may also be eating dirt or sand. If this is a chronic problem, have your child checked for anemia.

♥ IT IS NORMAL FOR
  · children to have gritty stools after eating some foods.

☞ SEE YOUR PEDIATRICIAN IF
  · your child is eating dirt or sand.

E. Little Brown Threads

What look like tiny, brown, nonwriggling worms in your child's diaper are probably undigested banana fibers. When I suggested this to one mother in my practice, she adamantly denied that her baby was consuming anything but breast milk. "Someone is giving her bananas," I said. The baby's grandmother finally admitted that she was sneaking in some mashed bananas when she babysat!

♥ IT IS NORMAL FOR
  · babies to have small brown threads in their stool after eating bananas.

F. Green

Some child care books tell you that green stools always mean something is wrong, but in my experience that is not true. Many children have a green stool once in a while without any apparent problem.

The green color may come from undigested bile. When stool travels rapidly through the gastrointestinal tract, there may not be enough time for digestive enzymes to break down green bile. This happens with diarrhea but also at odd times without any obvious cause.

Spinach, green drinks such as Gatorade or green Kool-Aid, lime gelatin, and some candies may also cause green stools.

♥ IT IS NORMAL FOR
* children to have an occasional green stool.

☎ CALL YOUR PEDIATRICIAN IF
* green stools are associated with diarrhea or other signs of illness.

G. White

White stools are usually caused by something your child ate—antacid tablets, or a barium solution for an x-ray, for example. Sometimes, however, a chalky white stool can be caused by hepatitis or some other liver problem. If that is the case, usually there will be jaundice (yellow discoloration of the skin and eyes) or other signs of illness.

♥ IT IS NORMAL FOR
* children to have pale or white stools after eating certain substances.

☞ SEE YOUR PEDIATRICIAN IF
* white stools persist.
* your child is also ill or jaundiced.

6 | ITCHY BOTTOM

The classical cause for anal itching in children is pin-worms. Tiny, white, half-inch-long, threadlike worms come out of the anus at night, lay microscopic eggs, then go back in. The eggs themselves itch, and the worms can tickle and itch when they go in and out.

If your child scratches at the anus and you cannot see a diaper rash or other irritation, wait until your child is asleep and look at the anus with a flashlight, gently spreading the buttocks. If you see worms, call your pediatrician in the morning and you will probably be given a prescription without having to go into the office.

If you do not see anything, you will have to bring your child in to be examined. Your pediatrician may instruct you in how to take a "tape test," pressing a piece of transparent tape against your child's anus first thing in the morning. Your doctor can then look at the tape under the microscope to see if there are any pin-worm eggs.

Your pediatrician may treat all family members, just the affected child, or all the younger children in your home.

Pinworms are so common among preschool-aged children that it is impossible to eradicate them from day-care and nursery schools. There is no need to inform the preschool or keep your child home because pin-worms, although uncomfortable, cause little or no dam-age.

Other causes for itching are a fissure or hemorrhoid, eczema, a yeast infection or another rash around the anus, or an infection or skin irritation following a bout of diarrhea.

☆ IT IS COMMON FOR
   •   children to have pinworms, which cause anal itching.

☎ CALL YOUR PEDIATRICIAN IF
- you see the pinworms.

☞ MAKE AN APPOINTMENT TO SEE YOUR PEDIATRICIAN IF
- there is no obvious cause for itching.
- you see a rash or irritation around the anus.

| 7 | VOMITING |

Just about every child vomits once in a while. A simple upset stomach can cause an episode of vomiting that is over as soon as the stomach is empty. Persistent vomiting, however, is another story.

A baby who "spits up," which is gentler and involves smaller amounts than vomiting, may be perfectly healthy. If your baby spits up a lot and is also not gaining weight well or has frequent lung infections or episodes of wheezing, a backup of stomach contents into the esophagus *(gastroesophageal reflux)* may be the underlying cause.

Vomiting may be symptomatic of a stomach virus, especially if diarrhea accompanies the vomiting. If your child ever has a fever along with vomiting, however, more serious possibilities such as kidney infections or meningitis must be ruled out, so see your pediatrician immediately.

A child who vomits green or yellow liquid or who has a distended, hard, or tender abdomen should be seen immediately.

Vomited material that looks like coffee grounds may be partially digested blood from bleeding in the stomach.

A blow to the abdomen can produce swelling of the wall of the intestine a week or so after the injury. If your child was wearing a seat belt during an auto accident or was hit in the stomach and starts vomiting a few days after an injury, take your child to your pediatrician or to an emergency room.

Babies under four months—especially at four to six weeks of age—who vomit forcefully without acting sick and who are hungry again immediately may have *pyloric stenosis,* a common condition in which the muscle at the far end of the stomach grows abnormally large and prevents stomach contents from entering the intestine.

Babies with pyloric stenosis often have projectile vomiting—their stomach contents shoot several feet across the room. Any baby may have an occasional episode of projectile vomiting, but if it persists, see your pediatrician. Dehydration may develop if pyloric stenosis is not remedied promptly with a simple surgical procedure.

After an episode of vomiting, let your child's stomach rest for a while. I hear from parents all the time that their child vomited and they immediately gave the child something to drink, only to have that come up also. If you try to feed your child immediately, the chances are great that nothing will stay down.

With an infant, wait the normal period between feedings and then try a little bit of oral electrolyte solution such as Pedialyte, Lytren, or Ricelyte (available without a prescription in most pharmacies and some markets). Breastfed babies may continue to receive breast milk.

For older children, let them tell you when they feel like taking something and then limit the first feedings to small amounts of clear liquids—apple juice or flat ginger ale, for example.

If diarrhea accompanies vomiting, the risk of dehydration is increased, especially in infants.

☎ CALL YOUR PEDIATRICIAN IF

- vomiting seems to happen whenever your child drinks milk.
- diarrhea accompanies the vomiting.
- your infant spits up or vomits some feedings each day.
- your child vomits occasionally and appears to be losing weight.

☞ SEE YOUR PEDIATRICIAN *IMMEDIATELY* IF

• your baby is under four months and vomiting is projectile.

• vomiting is accompanied by fever.

• your child vomits yellow or green liquid or brown material that looks like coffee grounds.

• your child's stomach is hard, tender, or bloated.

• vomiting begins within a week or two following an injury to the stomach.

• there are any signs of dehydration: sunken eyes, dry mouth, no urine for six to eight hours, poor skin color and texture, no tears with crying.

• vomiting continues for more than a few hours and even clear liquids will not stay down.

• your child vomits without taking anything by mouth (dry heaves).

| 8 | COLIC |

Colic is defined as periods of inconsolable crying in an otherwise healthy infant under four months old. Normal babies cry a total of about 2¾ hours per day; colicky babies may cry more than three hours on most days. I tell parents that they know their child has colic if they have an irresistible urge to get him his own apartment.

Colic is really a symptom rather than a disease. Just as fever can be from many different causes, colic is probably caused by several different problems.

For generations people have believed that colic is caused by pain. Babies with colic will scream, draw up their legs, get red in the face, and tense up their bellies. Since this is what babies do when they are in pain, it is a natural assumption that colic involves pain. Evidence now suggests, however, that something else causes the hysterical, heart-wrenching crying.

Allergy or sensitivity to formula or cow's milk protein in mother's milk has been suggested as a cause, and indeed, in a small number of babies, changing formula or eliminating milk from the mother's diet will ease the problem. However, babies who are sensitive to cow's milk protein will almost always have some other symptom such as vomiting, diarrhea, blood in the stools, or poor weight gain.

Many people think that colic comes from gas pains, because babies often do pass gas while they are crying. The truth is, however, that all babies have gas, and there is no evidence that infants with colic have any more gas than other babies.

Parents, especially first-time parents, often feel responsible but your nervousness or inexperience is not the cause of colic. On the contrary, it is colic that causes anxiety and feelings of inadequacy in even the most experienced parents.

Although the cause of colic has not been discovered, it appears that crying decreases in frequency and duration when parents approach their colicky baby in a systematic way. Babies cry because they need something—food, holding, sucking, stimulation, or sleep, but what your baby needs at any given time may be a mystery. By the time you hit on what it was your baby was asking for in the first place, she may be so agitated and hysterical that even doing the right thing has no effect. For example, you may feel that your baby could not be hungry since she ate a half hour before. By the time you offer a feeding after trying walking, bouncing, changing, and burping, the baby is so upset that the nipple is refused.

The most important first step is to make sure that your baby is indeed not sick or in any pain. That means a thorough history and physical examination by your pediatrician to rule out some source of pain.

Your pediatrician should also be willing to see you every few weeks until colic disappears on its own. An infant whose physical examination was normal a few weeks ago may now have a source for pain—hard stool impacted in the bowel, for example, which was missed or not present before.

Your pediatrician should also help you formulate a systematic approach to relieve your baby's distress as well as reassure you that your baby is healthy.

Parents of colicky babies often need a "rescuer" who can take over temporarily and permit the worn-out caregivers to get away and recoup, if only for an hour. Remember, first of all, the sitter only has to deal with the crying for a short time, so do not feel guilty for leaving him or her with the baby.

Also, remember that no matter what you do, colic is over by the age of four months and your baby will be happy as a clam as though nothing had gone wrong.

☞ SEE YOUR PEDIATRICIAN IF

• your baby is crying excessively—to make sure nothing physical is wrong.

• colic persists beyond four months.

☞ KEEPING BUGGING YOUR PEDIATRICIAN OR GET ANOTHER OPINION IF

• you have a feeling that something is wrong.

9	UMBILICAL HERNIA
	(OUTIE BELLY BUTTON)

The belly button is formed from the hole in a baby's abdominal wall through which blood vessels traveled between baby and mother during fetal life. Most people's belly buttons are "innies," ones that look like little cups. A belly button that pouches outward, otherwise known as an "outie," results when this hole is larger than average. Sometimes it sticks out all the time; sometimes it only appears when the baby cries. Outies are painless and normal.

Outies are most common in African-American, Asian, and Native American babies, but can occur in any race. It is not caused by the way the umbilical cord was cut; the hole was there before the baby was born, even though you may not notice it until your baby is a few weeks old.

Through the centuries, all sorts of home remedies have been suggested—binding the belly or taping a quarter over the hernia, for example. The worst idea I ever heard is not to let the baby cry so that the outie stays in. Just try to do that!

There is nothing that you can do to make it go away before it goes away by itself. In the vast majority of cases, outies become innies by the end of childhood. If your child is one of the few who still have an outie by age ten to twelve and he finds it embarrassing, it can be surgically corrected.

♥ IT IS NORMAL FOR

- many children to have an umbilical hernia (outie) during childhood.

☞ CALL YOUR PEDIATRICIAN IF

- the condition persists beyond age ten and it bothers your child.
- if the bump becomes rock hard and painful and your child begins to vomit. (This is an extremely rare complication similar to when a groin hernia becomes stuck. I have never seen it happen but it is theoretically possible.)

CHAPTER V

Urine & Genitals

| I | **URINATION** |

A. Frequent

Babies urinate a lot, so what seems too much may be normal for age. Urine frequency decreases as children grow older:

AGE	AVERAGE FREQUENCY (PER 24 HOURS)
Infants up to 6 months	20
12 months	16
2 year olds	10
Adolescence to adulthood	4–6

Diabetes can cause frequent urination. Usually children with diabetes have had a gradual increase in urinary frequency over several days along with an associated increase in thirst and hunger even though they are losing weight. Children who were dry all day start having accidents, children who were dry all night suddenly start wetting the bed, and older children who slept through the night need to get up to urinate.

Some foods and drugs such as caffeine-containing drinks, antihistamines, and some asthma medications may speed up the kidneys to produce urine faster than usual.

A bladder infection can make a child urinate more often, although the actual amount of urine passed each time may be only a dribble. Usually bladder infections are accompanied by pain with urination and fever, but not always.

A child who develops a hankering for a lot of apple juice or goes on a Popsicle binge may urinate more often than usual merely as a response to an increased intake of fluids.

Rarely, excessive urination may be caused by some hormone problems or kidney disturbance which impairs the kidneys' ability to concentrate urine.

Also low on the list but still a consideration is anxiety or an involuntary attempt at getting attention. The birth of a sibling, moving, an upcoming trip—any change may provoke enough anxiety to stimulate a child to more frequent urination. A crucial difference with psychologically versus physically caused urine frequency is that psychologically associated problems usually do not disturb sleep.

Children with *obsessive-compulsive disorder* (see page 243) who have a fear of contamination may say they need to urinate in order to wash their hands repeatedly. Make sure it really is urination and not handwashing that is drawing your child to the bathroom.

♥ IT IS NORMAL FOR
- children to urinate more frequently after an increased intake of fluids, in association with certain foods or drugs, or as a response to stress or anxiety.

☞ SEE YOUR PEDIATRICIAN IF
- frequency persists more than a day or two.
- your child is awakening at night to urinate or

wetting the bed when this hasn't happened for a long time.

- frequency is associated with pain or fever.
- there is also an increase in appetite and thirst and a possibility of weight loss.

B. Painful

Painful urination is often accompanied by increased frequency and a sense of urgency.

Painful urination can mean a bladder or kidney infection, and as a matter of fact, pediatricians assume that is the case until tests prove otherwise. One out of twenty girls will have a urinary tract infection before puberty, so be sure your daughter's urine is examined anytime her urination hurts. Dark brown or red urine, fever, back pain, and wetting accidents are additional signs that you may be dealing with an infection, but sometimes burning or pain is the only clue.

The more dilute urine is, the less likely it is to hurt, so encourage your daughter to drink lots of fluids. Also, a handy trick to make urination more comfortable until you can see the doctor is to have your daughter urinate in a tub of warm water. This may sound yukky but it feels better.

Painful urination in girls can be caused by irritation of the bladder or urethra (the tube leading from the bladder to the outside) from bubble bath. This chemical irritation can also be caused by shampoo in the bathwater or soap left on the vagina after washing. Soap or bubble bath breaks down the protective mucus which lines the vagina and bladder, setting up irritation and causing symptoms similar to a urinary tract infection. Chemical irritation will not usually cause a fever, but it is difficult for your pediatrician to be sure that this is not an infection without checking a urine specimen.

To avoid chemical irritation, do not use bubble bath, wash your daughter's hair at the end of a bath instead of at the beginning, limit baths to fifteen minutes, and do not allow soap to float around. Having your daughter urinate immediately after bathing helps clear the area of chemicals, also.

Girls who wipe themselves hastily after using the toilet or who wipe from back to front rather than front to back can spread bacteria from stool over tender vaginal tissue. Sitting in a sandbox can also irritate the area and make urination painful.

Painful urination in a boy is of more concern. Although he may just have a simple irritation of the urethra from a viral infection or local irritation because of pressure, a urinary tract infection in a boy has more chance of being associated with serious abnormalities of the urinary tract than it does in a girl. For that reason, urine infections in boys must be investigated, diagnosed, and treated early and completely.

Occasionally boys may develop painful urination because of irritation of the urethra (the tube that leads from the bladder to the outside through the penis) by their bike seat. This is especially common after Christmas when your son may have ridden his new bike with unaccustomed frequency. This diagnosis will only be made, however, after your pediatrician is sure there is no sign of infection in the urine.

♥ IT IS NORMAL FOR
- girls to have difficult or painful urination after bathing with bubble bath.

☎ CALL YOUR PEDIATRICIAN IF
- there is any painful urination in a boy.
- painful urination in a girl lasts longer than twelve hours or comes and goes over a few days.

☞ SEE YOUR PEDIATRICIAN *IMMEDIATELY* IF
- pain is severe.
- fever is over 101°F or your child has chills.
- abdominal or back pain accompanies painful urination.

- urine becomes bloody, cola-colored, or milky.
- your child looks sick along with having painful urination.

C. Straining

Straining with stool is common and may often be normal, but straining with urination is another story. It is always abnormal and must be brought to your pediatrician's attention immediately.

In boys, a malformation called posterior urethral valves, in which misplaced tissue formed before birth prevents the normal flow of urine out of the bladder, can cause straining with urination. If it is not corrected surgically, pressure from backup of urine gradually destroys kidney tissue. The earlier this is diagnosed, the better the chance of saving kidney function.

Other possible causes for straining to urinate are a kidney or bladder stone, a tumor, or a narrowing in the urinary tract. If the opening at the end of the penis is too small, your son may have a slow or dribbling stream of urine or an abnormally thin urine stream.

Whatever the reason, straining to urinate must always be investigated for an underlying cause.

⊗ IT IS **NOT** NORMAL FOR
- children to strain to urinate.

☞ SEE YOUR PEDIATRICIAN IF
- there is any sign of straining at any age.
- there is an abnormally thin or dribbling stream with or without straining.

D. Dribbling

Infection or a malformation in the lower urinary tract, irritation of the urethra (the tube leading from the bladder to the outside), or a neurological problem af-

fecting the bladder may cause a weak stream and dribbling.

Children who dribble out tiny bits of urine all the
time and have constantly damp underwear develop skin
rashes as well as a constant odor of urine around themselves.

⊗ IT IS **NOT** NORMAL FOR
- children to dribble urine.

☞ SEE YOUR PEDIATRICIAN IF
- there is any dribbling of urine.

| 2 | CHANGE IN URINE |

A. Strong Odor

Strong or strange urine odors can come from
certain foods, particularly asparagus; medications such
as penicillin and ampicillin; or mild dehydration from a
fever, overexertion in hot weather, or poor fluid intake
because of an upset stomach. Urine that remains in diapers for a long time may smell like ammonia. Most of
the time, urine odor is not caused by anything harmful
and disappears within twenty-four hours.

Infection can cause a foul smell, and some metabolic
abnormalities are associated with peculiar urine odors.
For example, an infant's urine that smells like sweaty
socks or maple syrup may signal disorders of protein
metabolism which can affect the brain.

If the odor persists after you've made sure your child
has taken a goodly amount of water or other fluids, if
the urine is discolored, or if your child is acting sick,
be sure to see your pediatrician promptly to rule out a
urinary tract infection.

♥ IT IS NORMAL FOR

· urine to smell strongly after certain foods, medications, or decreased fluid intake.

☞ SEE YOUR PEDIATRICIAN IF

· the smell persists after adequate fluid intake.

· there is discoloration along with the odor.

· your child has had neurological problems or slow development.

· strong odor is associated with frequent or painful urination.

· your child is acting sick.

B. Abnormal Colors

i. Red or Mahogany

A pink, red, or brown discoloration to the urine can be caused by dye in colored fruit drinks, beets, or even the coloring in a liquid medication. Blackberries, vegetable dyes, a chemical called phenolphthalein present in some over the counter laxatives, and infection with a bacteria called *Serratia marcescens* may also cause red urine.

Injured muscle can impart a mahogany color to the urine. A crushing injury in an auto accident, extreme muscle spasm such as occurs with a *grand mal convulsion,* or illness such as severe asthma or even a bad case of *mononucleosis* can break down muscle tissue. If accompanied by bouts of abdominal pain, burgundy or mahogany-colored urine may be a sign of a metabolic disorder called *porphyria.*

Blood in the urine may signal a urinary tract infection or a kidney stone, especially if associated with abdominal, back, or pelvic pain. Although more common in adults, kidney stones are not unheard of in children.

A blow to the back can cause bleeding into the kidneys, but sometimes not until a few days later.

ii. Pink, Orange, or Red-Brown

Beets, blackberries, some medicines for control of seizures, phenolphthalein in laxatives, and two drugs used infrequently in children—rifampin and pyridium—may turn urine orange to red-brown or pink.

iii. Blue or Green

Urine may turn blue or green because of vegetable dyes, such as the decorations on birthday cakes, for example. One of my patients had bright blue urine after eating a cupcake with a Cookie Monster made of blue frosting on the top. One of the chemicals in certain laxatives can turn urine blue. Color may vary depending on the acidity of the urine, so you might see the color only intermittently.

Infection with a bacteria called pseudomonas and an inherited disorder which causes elevated calcium and kidney stones may also color urine blue.

iv. Black

With an inherited metabolic disorder called *alcaptonuria,* urine turns black after it is exposed to the air. Diapers may appear normal immediately after urination but a little while later take on a black stain. This is not a serious disease but may cause some complications later in life, so it is helpful for the diagnosis to be made in infancy.

Medicine for pinworms (metronidazole), rhubarb, and senna can also turn urine black.

v. Dark, Amber

Dark, amber-colored urine may simply mean that your child has not had enough fluid, although persistently dark urine may come from kidney inflammation. Dark urine that is the color of strong tea may accompany *hepatitis*.

Children are often reluctant to produce a urine specimen in a strange bathroom. If you can, collect a fresh specimen just before you leave home in a clean container and bring it to your pediatrician.

It is best to bring in fresh, unrefrigerated urine, but if it will be more than an hour before you bring it in, refrigerate the specimen to prevent bacteria from growing. Crystals can form in cold urine and make it cloudy, but the crystals dissolve when the doctor warms it again.

♥ IT IS NORMAL FOR

• children to have pink, red, brown, blue, or amber urine under certain circumstances, although it should be checked.

☎ CALL YOUR PEDIATRICIAN IF

• your child is well and you cannot account for the discoloration.

☎ CALL YOUR PEDIATRICIAN *IMMEDIATELY* IF

• there is obviously blood in the urine.
• there was a recent injury to the back associated with a change in urine color.
• there is a headache along with the discolored urine.
• eyelids, hands, or feet are puffy.
• your child is acting sick or complaining of pain in the back, side, abdomen, or with urination.
• abnormally colored urine is associated with a fever.

C. Clear Beads or Granules in the Diaper

Superabsorbent disposable diapers are made with a nontoxic gel that absorbs an enormous quantity of urine, which helps to keep babies' skin dry. Sometimes this gel oozes through the top layer of the diaper, and forms tiny, clear beads. This material is not toxic to your baby.

♥ IT IS NORMAL FOR

· superabsorbent diapers to discharge little clear beads on the surface of the diaper.

D. Cloudy or Milky

Milkiness or cloudiness when urine is at room temperature may be caused by pus cells from a urinary tract infection. The chance of infection is increased if urine is also foul-smelling.

Cloudiness may also come from crystals that form in urine which is prone to forming kidney stones. Often there is a family history of stones in children whose urine is persistently filled with crystals. Phosphate crystals which are not necessarily associated with kidney stones can form in alkaline urine. They disappear when the urine is diluted by drinking more fluids or made more acid by what your child drinks.

Children who are dehydrated from vomiting and diarrhea, by a high fever, or through prolonged exposure to the heat may produce cloudy urine, but it will clear up once they start drinking again.

If you collect a urine specimen and keep it in the refrigerator until you go to the doctor, crystals may form, turning urine cloudy, but it will return to its normal appearance after warming.

♥ IT IS NORMAL FOR

· children to have cloudy or milky urine after it sits in the refrigerator or after a period of inadequate fluid intake.

☎ CALL YOUR PEDIATRICIAN IF

· cloudiness is associated with fever, painful urination, back or abdominal pain, frequent urination, new night or daytime wetting, or a bad smell.

· cloudiness persists after fluid intake increases.

- cloudiness is frequent and there is a history of kidney stones in the family.

---

3 | BEDWETTING

A. Chronic (Primary)—Child Has Never Been Dry at Night

Even though the majority of children are toilet trained by age three, almost one half of all three-year-olds and 10 percent of all six-year-olds still wet at night. Ninety-seven percent of all children are dry by age ten. Bedwetting over age six is more common in boys than girls, and often runs in families—uncles, aunts, and cousins as well as parents.

Three quarters of all adults with a history of childhood bedwetting have children who wet the bed, and these children often continue to wet until the same age as when their parent stopped wetting.

Bedwetting is not caused by emotional problems, but vigorous attempts to control this natural process may *cause* emotional problems. Wetting at night may or may not upset your child, but it does make most children reluctant to sleep over with a friend—unless that friend is a bedwetter also, of course!

Daytime wetting, which causes more social problems for children than nighttime wetting, is less common but more disruptive to everyday life. A child who wets *only* during the day may be dealing with an emotional problem.

If bedwetting or daytime wetting are associated with chronic or recurrent constipation, abdominal pain, soiling with stool, dribbling of urine, or a change in walking or coordination, there may be a more serious underlying problem. Constant dripping and persistently wet underwear may also signal a medical problem.

Whether you need to do anything to treat bedwetting, especially if there is a family history that suggests it will go away by a certain age, depends on how much it is disturbing your child. Treatments range from medications and alarm systems to behavior modification and hypnotic suggestion techniques. None of these is a permanent cure. When treatment is stopped, bedwetting usually recurs. It may be reasonable, however, to try some of these methods if concerns about bedwetting are making your child's life unhappy and reassurance that it will go away does not seem to be enough or it inhibits your child's social life—by causing reluctance to accept invitations for slumber parties, for example. (Actually, I always thought they should be called "awake parties," since the children giggle until the wee hours of the morning.)

♥ IT IS NORMAL FOR

· children to wet the bed at night until ages six to ten and for some children to wet during the day as well.

☎ CALL YOUR PEDIATRICIAN IF

· bedwetting never occurred before or stopped for a long time and restarted (see "Bedwetting as a New Problem," below).
· your child wets both day and night.
· there is pain or burning during urination.
· your child is twelve or over and still wetting.
· bedwetting is ruining the quality of your child's life.
· your child's underwear is constantly damp with urine.

B. A New Problem (Secondary)

If your child was previously able to stay dry at night and starts wetting all of a sudden, one of several conditions may be the cause: urinary tract infection, diabetes or other hormone problems, or emotional disturbance are the most common.

Although it may not be serious, the new onset of nighttime wetting should always be checked out.

⊗ IT IS **NOT** NORMAL FOR

· a child who was previously dry to start wetting the bed at night.

☞ SEE YOUR PEDIATRICAN IF

· any new bedwetting or daytime accidents begin.

4	GENITALS

A. Both Boys and Girls

i. *Injuries*

Girls can injure their vagina by falling on the cross bar of a boy's bike or onto a protruding object such as a sprinkler head. Boys often either catch their penis in a zipper or drop the toilet lid on it. Also, in the course of rough play, boys can be kicked in the groin, leading to bruising and swelling of the scrotum (the sack that holds the testicles) or penis.

By the way, if your son's penis is caught in a zipper and you cannot free it easily, leave it as is and go to the doctor's office or an emergency room. Once the tissue is firmly caught, the teeth of the zipper can be opened with a sharp object, but an upset parent and child struggling to do that at home may lead to further injury.

Treat bleeding in the genital area the same way you would treat bleeding anywhere else—apply pressure with a clean cloth and wash with soap and water after the bleeding stops. What looks like a major injury while it is bleeding may be only a tiny cut.

Most minor injuries do not damage a girl's hymen, but if bleeding seems to be coming from inside or if the injury might have penetrated the vagina, see your pediatrician immediately.

Swelling in other areas of the body can be minimized with ice, but this area is so sensitive that often an ice pack is not easily tolerated.

Make sure that your child can urinate normally after a genital injury.

☆ IT IS COMMON FOR
- children to injure the genital area.

☎ CALL YOUR PEDIATRICIAN IF
- the bleeding will not stop after five to ten minutes of pressure.
- your child cannot pass urine easily.
- the injury could have penetrated the vagina or there was bleeding from inside the vagina.
- your boy's scrotum is still swollen and painful a few hours after the injury, especially if pain is increasing rather than decreasing.
- there is blood in the urine or difficulty urinating.

ii. Groin Swelling, Hard and Soft

"Groin" refers to the area that lies above the crease between the leg and the trunk and extends diagonally from the hip to the genitals.

Lumps in the groin area can be swollen lymph nodes, hernias, or a testicle or ovary in an abnormal position.

This area is rich in lymph nodes ("glands"), which can swell up when your child has an infection. They can remain enlarged for long periods just like the ones in the neck (see page 66). A lymph node in the groin can be as small as a green pea or reach the size of a walnut or even larger. A swollen lymph node should move under your hand when you feel it, it should not be tender (although it often tickles when you try to feel that area), and the skin over it should not be discolored or red. If it is rock hard, firmly immovable, or red and tender, see your pediatrician.

Where *is* the groin?

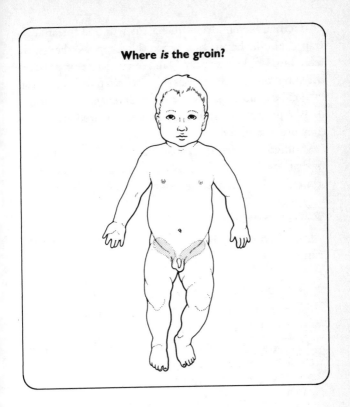

Another cause for groin swelling is a hernia, which involves the protrusion of intestine and some other abdominal tissues through a defect in the wall of the abdomen. In boys the swelling leads into the scrotum; in girls it forms a mass over one side of the pubic area. It feels squishy and soft and is usually oval or sausage-shaped. It may come and go, becoming more obvious when your child is standing up or crying and disappearing when your child is sleeping or relaxed.

Hernias are more common in boys than in girls, but both sexes have them. One out of three of the smallest preemies and one out of every one hundred boys develops a hernia. Hernias in children do not come from straining as they sometimes do in older people but result from lack of closure of a tube before birth.

Hernias in children are painless unless intestine is trapped in the hernia sac. When this happens, the hernia feels hard, looks discolored, and hurts. More important, the trapped intestine causes a bowel obstruction, which can make children seriously ill or can even be fatal if not treated promptly. Hernias should be repaired soon after they are diagnosed.

Sometimes in girls, an ovary slides into the hernia. In that case, the swelling resembles a lymph node, and sometimes a biopsy is necessary to tell the difference.

♥ IT IS NORMAL FOR

· children to have some swollen glands in the groin.

☎ CALL YOUR PEDIATRICIAN IF

· the swelling is rock hard, discolored, or tender, or if your child is vomiting.

· there are many swollen glands or the swelling is large or comes and goes.

· if you think there is a hernia.

· if you think the swellings are just swollen glands but do not diminish in a week or two.

B. Boys

i. Asymmetrical Scrotum; One Testicle Higher Than the Other; Disappearing Testicle

You may notice while bathing your boy that all of a sudden there appears to be either only one testicle or both are missing. The more you feel around to find them, the more likely they are to retract even further.

Little boys' testicles are attached to highly sensitive muscles that can pull them up into the body so that they virtually disappear. This happens with cold or embarrassment, and when other people touch them.

The best time to check that your son's testicles are in a normal position is when he is sitting relaxed in a warm bath or playing in a warm room with his diaper off. It is not impossible for a testicle which used to be down in the scrotum to retract permanently, but this is usually because a hernia or hydrocele closes and pulls the testicle up with it.

♥ IT IS NORMAL FOR
· a boy's testicles to be asymmetrical.
· testicles to retract and become invisible under certain circumstances.

☞ SEE YOUR PEDIATRICIAN IF
· you notice that one or both sides of the scrotum seem to be empty all the time.
· one side of the scrotum appears better developed with a larger amount of tissue than the other.

ii. Swollen Scrotum

Painless swelling in the scrotum can be caused by a hernia or a hydrocele.

A hydrocele is a painless collection of fluid above the testicle that is often present at birth. It may take most of the first year to clear up.

If the swelling changes, growing bigger and smaller from time to time, or seems to go away and come back, you may be dealing with a hernia (see page 133).

Painful swelling of the scrotum, on the other hand, is more serious. Torsion (or twisting) of the testicle, infection, or inflammation of the testicle or of one of the structures around it can cause scrotal pain.

Pain in the scrotum can come from inflammation or infection of the testicles or lymph nodes, or an infection of the skin of the scrotum.

A severe diaper rash can lead to a scrotal skin infection with swelling.

After a kick or a blow to the scrotum, pain should diminish and virtually disappear in a few hours. If pain persists or if it increases rather than decreases, bleeding or some more serious tissue damage may have occurred.

♥ IT IS NORMAL FOR

· infant boys to have painless hydroceles which take many months to go away.

⊗ IT IS **NOT** NORMAL FOR

· boys to have pain in the scrotum or testicles.

☎ CALL YOUR PEDIATRICIAN IF

· the swelling changes size.
· the swelling is painful to the touch, there is redness or discoloration, or the testicles hurt.
· the swelling was not there at birth.
· pain from an injury to the scrotum does not subside in a few hours.

☞ SEE YOUR PEDIATRICIAN OR AN EMERGENCY FACILITY **IMMEDIATELY** FOR

· sudden onset of severe pain in the scrotum or testicles.

iii. Swollen Penis

The penis can swell after an injury such as when your son drops the toilet lid on it. Infection can also cause swelling, and it is usually accompanied by redness and tenderness as well as discharge or oozing.

Wet diapers irritate the skin of the penis if they are left on too long. With a bout of diarrhea, liquid stool can burn the top layer of skin. Often this kind of swelling is confined to the end of the head of the penis, and it looks like there is a water-filled inner tube around it. This condition is not as painful as it looks, and it goes away in a day or so if you leave the diaper off and soak the penis in clear warm water a few times a day.

Long hairs that fall into the diaper can wrap around the penis. As the hair digs into the skin, sharply demarcated swelling and redness develop. The hair is usually difficult if not impossible to see once swelling obscures it. Allowed to continue, blood supply to the tip of the penis may be cut off and permanent damage may result, so see your pediatrician right away if this happens.

⊗ IT IS **NOT** NORMAL FOR
- the penis to be swollen.

☞ SEE YOUR PEDIATRICIAN IF
- there is any swelling of the penis.

iv. Foreskin Stuck Behind the Head of the Penis

Some parents have been told that they should retract the foreskin behind the head of the penis in order to clean under it. This is not necessary.

There is no need to retract the foreskin any farther than it will go comfortably; forceful retraction is not only painful, but may cause complications. It may take as long as ten years before the foreskin fully retracts comfortably.

If the foreskin is retracted forcibly and it becomes lodged behind the head of the penis and cannot be replaced in its normal position, the foreskin swells in its "stuck" position, and forms a constricting ring. As the penis also swells, it becomes impossible to replace the foreskin over the swollen shaft.

This condition, called *paraphimosis,* requires corrective surgery as soon as possible.

♥ IT IS NORMAL FOR
- the foreskin to retract only partway until a boy is ten years old or more.

☎ CALL YOUR PEDIATRICIAN
- immediately if the foreskin is stuck behind the head of the penis.

v. Swollen Foreskin

Problems with the foreskin in boys are almost always the result of poor hygiene, although catching the foreskin in a zipper can do it. Soapy water left underneath the foreskin after washing may also cause irritation and swelling.

If your boy's foreskin is swollen but neither red nor uncomfortable, let him sit in warm water for fifteen minutes every few hours. Leave his penis open to the air and see if the swelling goes down by itself. If it does not, or if the foreskin is red and tender, see your pediatrician for treatment.

♥ IT IS NORMAL FOR

· the foreskin to swell when irritated or treated too forcefully.

☎ CALL YOUR PEDIATRICIAN IF

· there is pus, redness, pain, or fever associated with the swelling.
· urination is difficult.

vi. Waxy White Material Under the Foreskin

Waxy white material forms under the edge of the foreskin in a boy who is uncircumcised or in one who has been circumcised but in whom a small amount of foreskin tissue was left behind. This is not pus, and is not the same as the secretions grown men form in that area after puberty.

This noninfected, nonsmelly, whitish yellow material comes from the gradual separation of the base of the foreskin from the surface of the penis. You do not need to do anything about it. In fact, vigorous attempts to remove it will only cause pain, irritation, and possible infection.

♥ IT IS NORMAL FOR

· boys to form waxy white material under the edge of the foreskin.

☎ CALL YOUR PEDIATRICIAN IF

· the material is foul-smelling or not confined to the edge of the foreskin.
· there is redness or tenderness associated with it.

C. Girls

i. Vaginal Discharge

These days any vaginal problem is likely to raise fears of sexual abuse, but unless there is evidence of physical trauma such as tears or bruising, your pediatrician finds evidence of a sexually transmitted disease, or your daughter is exhibiting signs of emotional distress, the chances are low.

There are several reasons why a little girl's vagina is more susceptible to infection than a grown woman's:

· The lining of the vagina is thin before the female hormones that start circulating at puberty cause it to thicken and become more resistant to invasion by germs.

· The vagina is not protected by the thick labia and pubic hair that adult women have.

· The vagina is closer to the anus, which can be a source of bacteria.

· Children generally practice poorer hygiene than adults. Girls may scratch their bottoms with dirty hands, wipe from back to front or hurriedly and incompletely, and are less likely to change soiled underwear promptly.

Some common causes of vaginal irritation and/or discharge are:

· Sitting in bubble bath
· Wearing tight leotards or jeans
· Sitting for long periods in a wet bathing suit
· Playing in a sandbox
· Having a foreign body in the vagina

You may have noticed the absence of a yeast infection on that list because this is rare before puberty.

The same germ that causes strep throats or bacteria from the anus can cause yellow-green or watery white vaginal discharge. With a foreign body such as a wad of toilet paper in the vagina, the discharge is foul-smelling as well.

Pain may occur when urine passes over irritated vaginal tissue, and this mimics the symptoms of a urinary tract infection. Until you can see your pediatrician, encourage your daughter to drink extra fluids so that her urine is more dilute and less irritating. Urinating while sitting in a tub of clear, warm water often decreases discomfort considerably.

At the earliest beginnings of puberty—which in some girls is as early as nine and others not until twelve or later, a watery, clear vaginal discharge which does not itch, burn, or smell bad may intermittently appear on your daughter's panties. This is a normal harbinger of maturation.

♥ IT IS NORMAL FOR

· girls to have occasional vaginal infections and irritations.

· girls to have a watery, clear, nonitching discharge at the onset of puberty.

☞ SEE YOUR PEDIATRICIAN IF

· there is any discharge that looks like pus or blood.

· discharge is foul-smelling.

· vaginal problems are associated with emotional disturbance, signs of trauma, or any suspicion that your daughter may have been sexually abused.

☞ SEE YOUR DOCTOR *IMMEDIATELY* IF

· vaginal problems are associated with fever, bleeding, or any other signs of general illness.

ii. Vaginal Itching

Since vaginal tissue in little girls is so delicate, anything that can irritate skin anywhere else on the body can do it in spades to that area. Dyes and perfumes in toilet paper, chemicals in detergents and fabric softeners, and soap and bubble bath may cause itching.

Pinworms (see page 111) usually inhabit the anus and rectum, but can infest the vagina also. If you see pinworms around the anus and your daughter is scratching her vagina, it may be due to the worms.

☆ IT IS COMMON FOR
- little girls to have an itchy vagina from time to time.

☎ CALL YOUR PEDIATRICIAN IF
- you see or suspect pinworms.

☞ SEE YOUR PEDIATRICIAN IF
- you eliminate all the irritants you can think of and your daughter is still itching.
- there is a discharge associated with the itch.

iii. Vaginal Bleeding

The only time bleeding from the vagina may be normal before the onset of menstruation is in a newborn girl (see page 40). Any other bleeding before the normal time for menstruation to begin is cause for concern. Polyps, tumors, bleeding disorders, hormone problems, or injury must be ruled out.

⊗ IT IS **NOT** NORMAL FOR
- girls to have vaginal bleeding before puberty except for a small amount during the first week or two of life.

☞ SEE YOUR PEDIATRICIAN FOR
- any vaginal bleeding.

iv. Foreign Body in the Vagina

In the normal course of exploring their bodies, many children put objects into their noses, ears, and any other available orifice. I have treated girls who have put beads, crayons, and toilet tissue in their vagina. If this material is allowed to remain, infection can follow.

Do not try to remove a foreign body from your daughter's vagina yourself unless it has no sharp edges, is protruding, and is extremely easy to pull out. You run the risk of pushing it in farther or damaging tissues if you cannot remove it easily.

Sometimes an object can be removed in the pediatrician's office, but often it is necessary to consult a gynecologist to take it out.

♥ IT IS NORMAL FOR

- little girls to insert an object into their vagina—but no more than once.

☎ CALL YOUR PEDIATRICIAN *IMMEDIATELY* IF

- the object is sharp.
- there is bleeding or discharge.
- you cannot remove the object easily.

☎ CALL YOUR PEDIATRICIAN IF

- this happens repeatedly; sexual abuse or other causes of emotional upset may be the cause.

v. Labia Stuck Together (Labial Adhesions)

Between ages six months and six years, the labia (outside lips) of the vagina may stick together. Most often your pediatrician is the one who notices this, but sometimes mothers notice that "something looks funny" when they bathe their daughter. This may be a result of chronic irritation from diapers or vaginal inflammation, but usually it is just a normal occurrence in prepubertal girls. If your daughter does not have any discomfort, signs of infection, or trouble urinating, there is no need to do anything.

Under no circumstances should the labia be forcefully separated. Not only does that cause pain, but it does no good; they will just become stuck again. When female hormone levels rise at puberty, the labia will separate naturally.

If there are problems with vaginal infection, difficult urination, or dribbling from urine that gets trapped inside the area, your pediatrician may prescribe an estrogen cream for a few weeks followed by nightly applications of a mild lubricating cream to keep the labia open.

♥ IT IS NORMAL FOR

- girls to have labia that stick together before puberty.

☞ SEE YOUR PEDIATRICIAN IF

- your daughter is uncomfortable, has trouble urinating, or there are recurrent infections in that area.

CHAPTER VI

Skin Problems

I have always wished there were a way to look at a rash over the phone. When I talk to parents, their child's rash is almost always "red spots," and what I call welts they may call pimples. There are zillions of causes for children's rashes. Not only do many rashes look alike, but their descriptions even sound alike. Most of them are not serious, but sometimes a rash is an early sign of serious medical problems.

This chapter will not necessarily make you able to diagnose definitely whatever you might see on your child's skin, but you may find out what might be serious and what can wait for a scheduled appointment.

> ■ ANYTIME YOUR CHILD HAS A FEVER ALONG WITH A RASH, CONTACT YOUR PEDIATRICIAN IMMEDIATELY.
> ■ ANY RASH THAT INCLUDES AREAS OF PURPLE OR BLUE BRUISES MUST BE EVALUATED RIGHT AWAY.
> Either of these two symptoms may not be serious, but there is a chance they can signal meningitis, clotting problems, or other emergencies.

To evaluate your child's rash properly, undress your child completely and inspect the whole body. The rash that you think is only on the face may also be under the shirt or on the buttocks. Even if the rash does not look raised, run your hand over it to see if it is rough or raised from the surrounding skin. Press on it to see if the red skin blanches under pressure. Also check in the mouth, and on the palms and soles.

If you think you know what the rash might be, look it up in the alphabetical list of skin problems ("Rashes Described," pages 152–89) to see if you are correct.

If you are not sure what it might be, check the "Directory According to What the Rash Looks Like" on pages 146–51 and see if anything fits.

I haven't included everything that could possibly occur. As with any other medical problems in your child, see your doctor if your child looks sick or you are worried no matter what this chapter says.

• DIRECTORY ACCORDING TO WHAT THE • RASH LOOKS LIKE

I	DRY, SCALY RASHES

A. Dry skin with itchy, red scales

• Eczema (Atopic Dermatitis)—most pronounced in the elbow fold, behind the knees and ears, on the tops of the hands and feet, and in the scalp
• Seborrheic dermatitis—most obvious on the face, ears, and scalp

B. Well-delineated, red, raised areas with silvery scales on the back of the elbows, the front of the knees, the scalp, especially thick near the hairline, the fold of the buttocks, and around the nails:
• Psoriasis

C. A round, red, scaly ring on the trunk or back (which you may not have noticed), followed in one to thirty days by multiple, small, oval, red, nonitchy, scaly patches on the trunk and neck:

- Pityriasis rosea

D. One or a few separate, scaly, round, or oval patches anywhere on the skin that grow slowly, sometimes clearing in the center, sometimes remaining red and scaly throughout:

- Ringworm
- Eczema (Atopic Dermatitis)
- Pityriasis rosea
- Lyme disease

E. Scaly red rash (sometimes itchy) on the tops of the feet and toes or the ball of the foot and the bottoms of the toes:

- Shoe dermatitis
- Athlete's foot
- Eczema (Atopic Dermatitis)

F. Dry, flaky scalp

- Sebborheic dermatitis
- Fungal scalp infection
- Dandruff

---

2 | FLAT RASHES UNDER THE SKIN

A. Pinpoint red dots that do not blanch when you press on them, scattered in showers most commonly over the face, arms, and legs but can appear anywhere on the body:

- Petechiae

- B. Tiny red dots running together, especially dense in the groin, under the arms and around the neck, in skin folds or over joints, may or may not be slightly rough to the touch:
- Scarlet fever (scarlatina)
- Kawasaki disease
- Toxic shock

C. Small red dots that start on the forehead, then spread to the face, trunk, arms, and legs, accompanied by high fever, a barking cough, and red eyes:
- Measles (rubeola, ten-day measles, big measles).

D. A faint, slightly blotchy pink rash that starts on the face and spreads to the trunk and arms, disappears in forty-eight hours, with no fever, and slightly swollen glands around the ears or in back of the head near the neck:
- German measles, or rubella.

E. Flat, salmon-colored spots all over the body two to five days after a high fever:
- Roseola (infant measles).

F. Flat, pink, or salmon-colored spots, small or large, with normal skin in between, with or without fever or other signs of illness:
- Drug (medication) or viral rash.

G. Lacy rash under the skin most pronounced on the tops of the thighs and the outside of the arms; may or may not be accompanied by red cheeks with normal skin color around the mouth:
- Fifth disease *(erythema infectiosum)*.

3 | BUMPS AND BLISTERS,

WET AND DRY

A. Soft, yellow blister that softens, breaks, and oozes, forming a honey-colored crust; may or may not have red skin surrounding:
- Impetigo.
- Herpes simplex.

B. Red pimples that start on the trunk and develop small water blisters on top over twenty-four to forty-eight hours; after they break, crusts develop as new blisters form elsewhere; usually very itchy:
- Chicken pox.
- Flea bites.

C. Red pimples that develop tiny blisters on the top; clustered on only one or two areas of the body and do not change appearance radically over one to two days; sometimes slightly red skin around the base; might be itchy or not:
- Flea bites.

D. Painless round or oblong blisters on the palms, fingertips, soles of the feet, and the webs between the toes, sometimes on the trunk; painful blisters in the mouth may also appear:
- Hand, foot, mouth syndrome.

E. Painless, scattered, waxlike, colorless bumps mainly on the trunk but sometimes on the face, genitals, and groin with pinpoint pits in the center:
- Molluscum contagiosum.

F. Tiny red bumps most dense in the armpit, groin, and around the neck that feel like fine sandpaper:
- Scarlet fever
- Kawasaki disease.

G. Flesh-colored, rough bumps that are single, a few together, or in clusters on the hands, face, fingers, toes, soles of the feet, or knees:
- Warts.

---

4   RAISED RASHES

A. Raised red welts that have circular or wavy borders; sometimes run together, normal skin in between; each welt can last a few minutes to several days, and new ones form as old ones fade:
- Hives.
- Erythema multiforme.

B. Painful, tender red nodules on the shins or forearms:
- Erythema nodosum.

C. Tiny bumps or pimples on the skin between the fingers and toes, tops of the feet, elbows, armpits, and/or genitals; itchy:
- Scabies.
- Swimmer's itch, seabather's eruption.
- Atopic Dermatitis.

---

5   RASHES THAT FORM RINGS

A. Only one or two red rings with scaly edges, sometimes clearing in the center, sometimes remaining red:

- Ringworm.
- Pityriasis Rosea.
- Lyme disease (Erythema chronicum migrans).

---

6 | DIAPER RASHES

A. Red, chafed areas on the thighs, buttocks, and waist:
- Chafing dermatitis.

B. Bright red irritation around the anus:
- Anal rash (see "Diaper Rash," page 157).

C. Open ulcers on reddened skin in the diaper area and on the genitals:
- Ulcerating dermatitis (see "Diaper Rash," page 158).

D. Beefy red spots running together with small satellite spots:
- Fungal diaper rash (monilia, candida diaper rash).

---

7 | BIRTHMARKS

A. Bright, cherry red, raised marks anywhere on the body:
- Strawberry marks (capillary hemangiomas).

B. Brown or tan moles that are present at birth or develop during childhood:
- Moles.
- Café au lait spots, freckles.

· **RASHES DESCRIBED** ·

| 1 | ATHLETE'S FOOT |

Athlete's foot is a fungus (or yeast) infection that involves the weight-bearing portions of the foot—the sole, the instep, underneath and between the toes. Blisters on the instep, cracks between the toes, and redness and scaling are characteristic. It flares in hot, humid weather.

This occurs mostly in males and rarely before adolescence. Chances are that the scaly, itchy rash or dry cracking on your child's feet are caused by eczema or a reaction to shoes rather than athlete's foot (see "Shoe Dermatitis," page 185, and Eczema," pages 160–62). Nevertheless, children who wear athletic-type shoes all day with sweaty feet can develop this fungus even at a young age.

⊗ IT IS **NOT** NORMAL FOR
 · children to have athlete's foot before puberty.

☞ SEE YOUR PEDIATRICIAN IF
 · you think your child has athlete's foot. A scraping to identify the specific fungal infection and prescription medication may be necessary, although good over-the-counter medications such as Micatin and Lotrimin are often effective.

| 2 | CAFÉ AU LAIT SPOTS, FRECKLES |

Small to large, flat, light brown spots the color of coffee with cream are rarely present at birth, but begin appearing shortly after. Individual spots are not associated with any problems, but if your child has six or more of them and each is more than about three-quarters of an inch across, they may be a sign of *von Recklinghausen's disease*. This inherited disorder can affect hearing and other neurological systems.

Scattered, small brown freckles less than one-quarter inch or so that are most prominent in sun-exposed areas are common on the skin of light complexioned people. (Their presence is actually an indication that there may have been too much sun exposure.) However, large freckles on the trunk in the area under the arms which usually has little or no sun exposure and no freckles may also be a sign of von Recklinghausen's disease.

♥ IT IS NORMAL FOR

·   children to have some freckles in light-exposed areas.

·   children to have a few *small,* flat, light brown birthmarks anywhere on their bodies.

☞ SEE YOUR PEDIATRICIAN IF

·   your child has more than six café au lait spots.

·   freckles appear in areas that are not exposed to the sun.

| 3 | CHICKEN POX |

Chicken pox is usually a mild disease that causes a slight fever the day before pocks break out and for the first day or two after. Although most people seem to catch it sometime during childhood, some are exposed numerous times and never break out. The incubation period is ten to twenty-one days after exposure.

Spots appear first on the face and trunk and then spread to all areas of the body. Small red pimples develop a pinpoint water blister on the top which enlarges and sometimes appears to contain yellow material inside. New blisters continue to appear for three to five days while earlier ones are breaking, crusting, and drying up.

Pocks which form in moist areas of the body such as around the vagina and in the groin of a diapered infant may not crust over but remain weepy and look like open ulcers.

Chicken pox may be confused with flea bites at first, but flea bites do not multiply and change their appearance radically over one to two days as chicken pox do.

If you are sure your child has chicken pox, there is no need to see the doctor; you can simply call for directions on how to make your child more comfortable. In fact, I try to hustle children with chicken pox in and out by the back door of my office so they won't expose other children, especially those with chronic diseases who are more susceptible to the complications of chicken pox.

Chicken pox is contagious starting one or two days before the rash breaks out and persists until all the pocks are dry and crusted, a period of seven to ten days. Schools and most group day-care centers usually want you to keep your child home until all the sores are dry, although some doctors, myself included, think that it is enough to keep a child home just until no new pocks break out.

On rare occasions, children with chicken pox develop complications such as pneumonia or encephalitis. *Reye's syndrome,* a combination of liver failure and brain swelling, is a complication of chicken pox which is more likely to occur if children are given aspirin. If your child becomes excessively sleepy, difficult to arouse, or vomits while recovering from chicken pox, go to the hospital emergency room or your pediatrician's office immediately.

♥ IT IS NORMAL FOR

• enlarged lymph nodes to appear on the back of the head, on the neck, and in the groin while your child has chicken pox, and for a week or two afterward.

☆ THERE IS **NO NEED** TO SEE YOUR PEDIATRICIAN FOR

- routine chicken pox.

☎ CALL YOUR PEDIATRICIAN FOR

- advice about whether your child should receive a new medication to shorten the course of chicken pox.

☞ SEE YOUR PEDIATRICIAN IF

- your child seems to have a severe case, especially if there are zillions of pocks on the face.
- scabs drain pus.
- there is a large area of redness surrounding one or more pocks.
- a lymph node (gland) becomes red, tender, or extremely large.

☞ GO **IMMEDIATELY** TO YOUR PEDIATRICIAN'S OFFICE OR THE EMERGENCY ROOM IF

- your child develops a high fever, extreme tiredness, excessive sleeping, cough, confusion, vomiting, trouble breathing or walking, or any other signs of serious illness.
- there is redness and tenderness *around* a pock, especially if there is also a fever.

| 4 | CRADLE CAP (SEBORRHEIC DERMATITIS) |

Cradle cap and other related scaly rashes start between the second and tenth weeks of life. The scales on the scalp may be yellow and greasy-looking or dry and white, and they usually adhere tightly to the skin. They do not itch. Seborrheic dermatitis can also break out around the eyebrows, the forehead, and behind the ears.

Most cases of seborrheic dermatitis clear up in a few weeks to months without any treatment. If its appearance bothers you, however, your pediatrician can prescribe a cream or lotion.

Seborrheic dermatitis usually disappears in the period between eighteen months and the beginning of puberty, and then it may reappear. Therefore, what looks like dandruff in a child between two and twelve is probably not due to seborrheic dermatitis.

Severe seborrhea or cradle cap in an infant can, on rare occasions, be caused by serious underlying conditions called *histiocytosis* or *Letterer Siwe disease*. If simple treatment does not make it better, further testing may be necessary.

☆ IT IS COMMON FOR

· children between birth and eighteen months to develop seborrhea.

☎ CALL YOUR PEDIATRICIAN IF

· the rash is severe or simple measures do not improve the appearance.

· it spreads to other parts of the body.

· it is associated with weight loss, poor feeding, or diarrhea.

| 5 | DANDRUFF |

The dry, flaking, itchy scalp problem called dandruff can sometimes show up in children, most often in those with dry skin associated with eczema. It is more common, however, in adolescents and adults.

Over-the-counter dandruff shampoos often relieve the symptoms. If they do not, there is a possibility that your child has a fungal scalp infection (see page 166), especially if other people in the family are experiencing the same problem.

⊖ IT IS UNCOMMON FOR

· children to have dandruff before puberty.

☞ **SEE YOUR PEDIATRICIAN IF**

- simple treatment fails.

| 6 | DIAPER RASH |

All forms of diaper rash are caused in the first place by the same thing: prolonged contact of an infant's skin with urine and stool. Contrary to what many people still think, ammonia does not play much of a role. Disposable diapers, especially the superabsorbent kind, do keep children's skin dryer than cloth diapers can, but rashes can occur in children wearing either type.

Diaper rashes can develop overnight or in just a few hours. You might put your child to bed or down for a nap with clear skin and just a few hours later the skin is red and sore.

The ultimate cure for diaper rash is, of course, toilet training. Until your child is out of diapers, however, you will probably have to deal with rashes from time to time.

A. Anal Rash

Breastfed newborns with normal, loose, watery stools or older infants with diarrhea may develop a bright red rash around the opening of the anus. If this is oozing, crusty, or painful, and does not clear up with simple measures, it might be due to an infection of the skin caused by strep, the same germ that causes throat infections.

B. Chafing Dermatitis

In babies seven to ten months old, the volume of urine they pass increases dramatically and often exceeds the absorbing capacity of their diapers. Rough, red skin around the tops of the thighs and the waist results when skin rubs against the wet diaper.

C. Ulcerating Dermatitis

Throughout the diaper area, including the genitals, open ulcers can form in red, irritated skin. This rash is often painful when urine and stool touch it.

The most important treatment for all of these types of diaper rash is air and dryness; change diapers frequently or, better yet, leave them off for as long as you can at various times—making provisions for the inevitable consequences, of course. Your pediatrician will have specific recommendations for creams and drying regimens.

♥ IT IS NORMAL FOR

• babies in diapers to have rashes once in a while, no matter how conscientiously they are changed.

☎ CALL YOUR PEDIATRICIAN IF

• you need a plan of attack to clear up a simple diaper rash.

• you see loose, yellow, fluid filled blisters which may break open and leave raw areas; this might be a sign of staph infection and needs antibiotic treatment.

• there is oozing, crusting or pain from a bright red anal rash.

D. Fungal (Monilia, Candida, Yeast) Rash

A fungus or mold called monilia or candida lives on our skin and in our mouths all the time. When skin in the diaper area is wet or sore and normal protective barriers break down, the fungus can invade underneath the skin and set up an infection. A fungal diaper rash is dark pink and swollen-looking with small satellite spots around the edges. It looks angry, but oddly enough does not usually cause much discomfort to your baby. Because of its appearance, it often distresses parents more than it does infants.

Fungal diaper rashes are especially common when a baby has been taking antibiotics.

Fungal diaper rash may require a prescription cream to clear up, although over-the-counter creams such as Micatin or Lotrimin often work. It may recur quite easily and frequently as long as your baby is in diapers.

♥ IT IS NORMAL FOR

· infants to develop fungal diaper rashes, no matter how well they are cared for, and especially when they have been taking antibiotics.

☞ SEE YOUR PEDIATRICIAN IF

· you suspect a fungal diaper rash.

· the treatment your doctor recommends does not work in a few days.

· the rash spreads to other parts of the baby's body.

| 7 | DRUG OR VIRAL RASH |

Chicken pox, measles, herpes, and roseola are viral infections that cause specific and easily identifiable rashes, but there are many other, less well-known but common viruses that cause less distinctive ones. *Infectious mononucleosis,* for example, can cause a dramatic rash which looks like many other viral rashes and even like some drug reactions.

With a viral rash, flat, red, or salmon-colored spots may remain separate or run together, leaving normal skin in between. There is usually no itching, and some parts of the rash may have tiny bleeding points under the skin (petechiae), although generally the rash blanches (turns white) when you press on it.

Some drugs, especially amoxicillin, cause a similar rash. Further muddying the waters is the fact that many children are given antibiotics when they have a virus. When the rash breaks out, it is difficult to know whether it is from the medication or the infection.

Allergic reactions to medications cause itching; hives; swelling of the hands, feet, and mouth; or difficulty breathing. A simple drug rash does not cause any of these severe symptoms.

Even if it is caused by an antibiotic, this type of rash is not a sign of allergy, but a side effect of the medicine. Your child does not have to be labeled as allergic to it unless there are other associated symptoms.

♥ IT IS NORMAL FOR

· children to have rashes that are hard to diagnose precisely.

☞ SEE YOUR PEDIATRICIAN IF

· any rash is accompanied by a fever.
· a rash does not go away in a few days.
· it involves the lips and mouth.
· it causes areas of bruising, or is purple or violet-colored.
· the rash is painful or blistering.

---

8 | ECZEMA (ATOPIC DERMATITIS)

The itching, oozing, redness, scaling, and crusting of eczema may begin as early as one month or at anytime later in childhood. In an infant, the face, scalp, trunk, and outside of the arms and legs are most often involved, whereas older children have it on the feet and hands, the bend of the elbows, and behind the knees. Skin is generally dry and rough, even on the areas that are not broken out.

Often there is a family history of allergy such as asthma or hay fever or another family member who has had eczema as a child.

Itching is common and can be intense, and some children go through "scratching frenzies," particularly in the evenings or when they are perspiring. Infants too

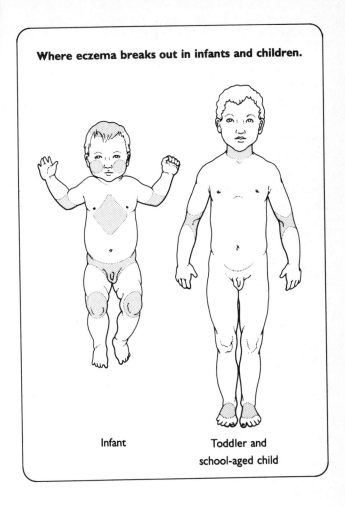

Where eczema breaks out in infants and children.

Infant

Toddler and
school-aged child

young to scratch may rub their faces on the sheets of
their crib. Although scratching brings temporary relief,
symptoms are often worse a short time later because of
chemicals in the skin that are released by scratching.

Many things can make eczema worse: wool or other
irritating fabrics, harsh detergents and soaps, jewelry
that contains nickel, certain foods, dry air, contact with
grass, even emotional stress. Also, anything that dries
the skin can make eczema worse.

Unfortunately, there is no cure, and it must go away
on its own. Eczema that starts early in infancy is usually

gone by age ten. If it starts later in childhood, it tends to be more long-lasting. Either type may wax and wane in a mild form throughout adulthood.

Your pediatrician can offer ways to make your child more comfortable: moisturizing the skin, avoiding irritants, giving medication by mouth to relieve itching, and applying cortisone-containing lotions, creams, or ointments.

Besides a child's misery, the major complication is the risk of skin infections from scratching with dirty fingernails.

☆ IT IS COMMON FOR

· many children to suffer from eczema (atopic dermatitis) during infancy and/or childhood.

☞ SEE YOUR PEDIATRICIAN IF

· you want to confirm the diagnosis. Especially in infants, many rashes mimic eczema, including scabies and seborrhea.

· the rash develops soft, yellow, oozing scabs, or red, tender areas, which can mean that eczema has become infected.

☎ CALL YOUR PEDIATRICIAN IF

· the itching interferes with sleep.

· you need a referral to a dermatologist if nothing you do alleviates the condition.

| 9 | ERYTHEMA MULTIFORME |

This rash may at first resemble hives or look like a viral rash. It changes daily over a five-day period as red patches on the arms and legs grow larger and start clearing in the center. Ringlike spots surrounding clear areas with round, red centers are called *target lesions* and are characteristic of erythema multiforme (which, literally translated, means "redness in many forms").

Often beginning on the tops of the arms and legs, the red spots gradually spread to the palms, soles, trunk, and even ears and mouth. They heal in two to four weeks, sometimes leaving behind temporary darkening or lightening of the skin.

In one third of all children, symptoms of a cold precede the rash, so at least in some cases it may be caused by a viral infection. This occurs frequently, for example, with herpes infections. Sometimes a drug—especially sulfa drugs, penicillins, and sedatives—causes it.

Severe reactions can lead to serious illness.

☆ IT IS COMMON FOR

- children to develop a rash which may be mild erythema multiforme after a viral infection or after taking certain drugs.

☎ CALL YOUR PEDIATRICIAN IF

- you suspect erythema multiforme.
- the rash is severe or progresses rapidly.
- your child is acting uncomfortable or sick.
- there is swelling or crusting of the mouth and lips or around the eyes.
- there is difficulty swallowing.
- your child is unable to urinate or urination is difficult.

---

10 | ERYTHEMA NODOSUM

Red, tender, painful lumps that appear on the shins and sometimes on the outer forearm may last two to six weeks. Sometimes the nodules on the legs are so painful they make children limp.

The condition is rare under age two and increases in frequency as children approach adolescence. In teenagers and adults it is often caused by oral contraceptives.

Erythema nodosum is usually either a response to certain infections or a reaction to medication. The nodules themselves do not require any treatment. They will go away, changing color as they do so like a bruise, turning purple, brown, then yellow. It is important to figure out whether the cause of it is something that requires treatment.

☞ SEE YOUR PEDIATRICIAN IF

· you suspect erythema nodosum for an exact diagnosis and to determine the cause.

| 11 | FIFTH DISEASE (ERYTHEMA INFECTIOSUM) |

Historically, the three most common childhood infections that caused a rash were measles, rubella, and scarlet fever. The fourth is not clear—perhaps one that never really existed, but erythema infectiosum has been designated the fifth. It strikes children between ages three and twelve, but usually not severely, provided they are healthy. On the other hand, children with sickle cell anemia, for example, may develop additional blood problems because of it.

The first stage looks as though someone slapped your child's cheeks, although bright red cheeks with normal-colored skin around the mouth may go unnoticed in a child who has naturally rosy cheeks.

By the second day, a spotty rash develops on the arms, legs, and trunk, which by the end of the first week looks like a lacy pattern under the skin. This last stage of the rash may come and go over several weeks, becoming more obvious after exposure to the sun or when your child is overheated.

Children with fifth disease are not sick and do not need to be kept home from school. The only danger is that in rare instances infection of a fetus can lead to blood problems before birth. A pregnant woman who is exposed to fifth disease should let her obstetrician know. Remember that a child may be contagious the day *before* the rash breaks out.

☞ SEE YOUR PEDIATRICIAN IF

• you need to confirm the diagnosis of fifth disease, especially if you are pregnant or you know your child exposed someone who is.

• your child has a fever over 101°F or is acting sick—it is probably something else.

---

12 | FLEA BITES

When fleas land on children, they bite several times in the same area. Medical textbooks refer to this as "breakfast, lunch, and dinner" because they tend to bite in groups of three. Since the bite may have a tiny blister on top, a crop of flea bites can often be confused with chicken pox, but flea bites do not break down into crusts as new ones break out. Also, flea bites are most common in exposed areas such as the arms and lower legs, or in areas where clothing is tight such as waistbands. Chicken pox, on the other hand, starts on the face, trunk, and back and then later spreads to the arms and legs.

Flea bites may or may not itch. Also, fleas may bite one person in a group or a family and leave others alone. Children are more prone to be bitten than adults because they are closer to the ground and more conveniently located for the fleas to jump onto. Children also tend to hug their flea-bearing pets more than adults do.

Flea eggs can live up to one year in carpeting, drapes, or upholstery; in the debris between floorboards; or in corners. Even if you do not have a dog or cat, your children can be bitten if you move into a home that used to contain a pet or if you visit someone with a dog or cat.

If your child was bitten in your own home, eliminate the fleas by fogging or spraying carpets, drapes, and upholstery and treating your pets.

☆ IT IS COMMON FOR

- some children to get flea bites and others not to.

13 | FUNGAL SCALP INFECTION

Ringworm used to be the most common scalp infection caused by a fungus, but that has changed.

This new type of scalp infection causes generalized scaling and flaking all over the scalp which looks a lot like dandruff except that there is often some hair loss also. Dandruff is uncommon in children before puberty, however, and usually responds quickly to over-the-counter dandruff remedies.

If you think your child has dandruff but simple treatment such as dandruff shampoos with coal tar or selenium do not clear it up, see your pediatrician. Looking at a scraping from the scalp under the microscope and/or a culture for fungus can make the diagnosis.

⊗ IT IS **NOT** NORMAL FOR

- children to have dandruff before puberty.

☞ SEE YOUR PEDIATRICIAN IF

- any dandruff persists after simple over-the-counter treatment.
- hair loss is associated with dandruff.

14 | GERMAN MEASLES (RUBELLA)

The faint pink rash of rubella starts on the face, then spreads to the trunk. By the time it reaches the forearms and lower legs, the face is clear. Usually children appear well, although they can have a slight fever for one to three days. Swollen glands in the area behind the ears or the back of the head are characteristic.

Rubella does not make children really sick and immunization with the MMR vaccine has reduced the incidence of this disease. The major risk occurs if a pregnant woman contracts the infection. Deafness, heart defects, or eye and brain problems in the baby can result.

☞ SEE YOUR PEDIATRICIAN
- to confirm the diagnosis.

| 15 | HAND, FOOT, MOUTH SYNDROME |

No, not hoof and mouth disease. Caused by a common virus called *Coxsackie,* this infection may cause mild fever, sore throat, or bellyache the day before the rash comes out, or there may be no preceding illness at all. Tiny oval or round blisters develop on the soles and edges of the feet, the palms of the hands and fingertips, and the webs of skin between the fingers and toes.

There is no treatment that helps, nor is any necessary, and the infection passes in a few days. Blisters and open ulcers in the mouth can be painful and may interfere with your child's ability to drink adequate amounts of liquid. In that case, acetaminophen (Tylenol, Tempra, etc.) or gels that you dab onto the sores such as Orajel or Numzit may help.

☞ SEE YOUR PEDIATRICIAN IF
- sores in the mouth are keeping your child from drinking enough liquids.

| 16 | HERPES SIMPLEX |

Herpes simplex is the virus that causes "cold sores," a painful collection of tiny blisters. Usually on the edge of the lip and inside the mouth, cold sores can involve the cheeks, chin, and nose as well as the hands and fingers. The virus is caught from family members or playmates who transmit the virus by touching, kissing, or sharing towels, toys, or eating utensils. The virus can be transmitted even before there is an open sore.

Herpes simplex virus is everywhere, and many people become infected with the virus during childhood without ever knowing it. Because they now have antibodies against it, they may never have a cold sore, even after direct exposure.

After the first sore heals, the herpes virus remains dormant in the body until exposure to the sun, a fever, or a cold reactivates it. Twenty percent of all children have repeated bouts of herpes, but subsequent infections are never as severe as the first one.

Herpes sores can resemble impetigo but they are different in several ways:

• There is often pain before herpes blisters break out, and the area is tender while the blisters form; impetigo usually does not hurt.

• the blisters of herpes simplex form a small, close circle with regular borders. Dermatologists call it "dew-drops on a rose petal"; impetigo enlarges and spreads asymmetrically and "messily."

• when the blisters of herpes break, they leave an open sore or a thin, clear crust, not the thick and honey-colored crust of impetigo.

Herpes infections are dangerous if they occur in newborns, in children who have impaired immunity—such as those being treated with cortisone or chemotherapy—or if they erupt on or around the eye.

Note: *This is herpes type 1, which is different from herpes type 2, the virus that causes genital herpes infections. They have similar names but are different.*

☎ CALL YOUR PEDIATRICIAN IF

• pain is not relieved by your usual pain medications.

• herpes infections keep coming back. There is a prescription cream or an oral medication that might shorten the duration and decrease the pain of recurrent herpes infections.

☞ SEE YOUR PEDIATRICIAN IF
• a herpes infection involves the eye.
• your child is on medicine that can impair immunity.
• you are not sure if it is herpes.
• the infection is so painful that your child will not take adequate fluids.

| 17 | HIVES (URTICARIA) |

Hives are red splotches or welts raised above the skin that have circular or wavy margins. They may come and go in minutes or over hours and may or may not itch. Attacks begin suddenly and can last one or two days or as long as several weeks.

After hives fade, they may leave behind a faint bluish discoloration for a day or two.

About 3 percent of all children have at least one episode of hives during their childhood. Hives are presumed to be an allergic reaction to food, medicine, or an infection, although in most cases the cause remains obscure.

The most common foods associated with hives are peanuts, eggs, nuts, beans, chocolate (boo-hoo), strawberries, tomatoes, condiments, fresh fruits, corn, fish (mainly shellfish), and pork. Also, food coloring and additives such as sulfites, MSG, and yellow dye No. 5 can cause them. Hives caused by a reaction to a food appear from ten minutes to eight hours after ingestion, depending upon where in the gastrointestinal tract the food is absorbed, so often it is difficult to pinpoint the guilty food. I broke out in hives as a child shortly after eating plum tomatoes, so my mother assumed my hives were due to that. My life without plum tomatoes was still rich and full, but I doubt they were the cause.

Drugs that most commonly cause hives are aspirin, penicillin (and its derivatives such as ampicillin), sulfa drugs, and codeine, although just about any medication can cause them. Even if a drug has been taken before without problems, it can still cause a reaction the next time it is used.

Some children develop hives with a strep infection or certain viral infections.

Exposure to cold, heat, pressure, sunlight, and stress can also cause hives but that is more common in adolescents.

In the vast majority of cases, even if you never figure out what caused them, the hives never return. Antihistamines are useful to relieve itching and sometimes to stop the reaction. Cortisone by mouth or by injection is also effective in severe cases.

♥ IT IS NORMAL FOR
   · children to have an episode of hives of unknown cause which never recurs.

☎ CALL YOUR PEDIATRICIAN IF
   · you think you know what caused the hives and wish to confirm your idea.
   · your child is uncomfortable and you need advice on what medicine to use.

☞ SEE YOUR PEDIATRICIAN IF
   · you are not sure your child's rash is hives.
   · there is swelling of the lips or eyelids, or your child has trouble breathing.
   · hives are accompanied by bruising, fever, or painful joint swelling.
   · hives keep recurring from time to time, especially after injuries, dental procedures, or exposure to cold.

18 | IMPETIGO

Impetigo is a bacterial infection of the skin caused most frequently by staph or strep germs. These bacteria live on our skin and in our mouths and noses all the time. When areas of the skin are irritated or broken, such as in the diaper area, the skin around the nose after a cold, or skin inflamed with chicken pox, these germs can invade and set up an infection.

Small pimples enlarge to one inch or more across, and form soft blisters filled with cloudy or yellow fluid. They then open and drain, forming a honey-colored crust as the sores continue to enlarge. Often new sores develop close by. Although herpes simplex produces small blisters that break and crust and may resemble impetigo at first, the blisters are clustered closer together and form a small, regular circle, while the borders of impetigo are usually irregular and larger.

Impetigo is more common when hygiene is poor, but if your child develops impetigo, it does not mean that you are a poor housekeeper. Even the cleanest children pick their noses with dirty hands, play in the dirt, and get cuts and scrapes all the time.

Impetigo must be treated with either oral antibiotics or a prescription cream, so your pediatrician needs to see your child. Treatment usually clears it up in about a week. If it is untreated, besides taking longer to clear up, it is more likely to leave scars.

☞ SEE YOUR PEDIATRICIAN FOR
- diagnosis and treatment of impetigo.

☎ CALL YOUR PEDIATRICIAN *IMMEDIATELY* IF
- the area around the impetigo becomes red and tender, especially if it is on the face.
- the sores continue to increase in size and/or number forty-eight hours after treatment is begun.
- fever develops.

19 | INFANT MEASLES (ROSEOLA)

Between about six months and two years, some children come down with an infection that drives parents and pediatricians nuts. An erratic fever—sometimes as high as 105°F—goes up and down for two to five days but your child may not seem terribly sick, especially when the temperature is down. During that time your pediatrician will not be able to find anything to account for the fever on examination, and may order blood tests, urinalyses, chest x-rays, sometimes even a spinal tap if the fever is extraordinarily high or if your child has a fever convulsion.

After the fever subsides, a rash breaks out, and everyone breathes a sigh of relief because now they know what the child *had*. Salmon pink spots under the skin appear all at once all over your child's body. They blanch if you press on them, and they do not itch.

The diagnosis of roseola may be difficult if your child had no fever or only a slight one before the rash appeared. In that case, your pediatrician may simply call it a "viral rash," and if your child was given antibiotics during the fever, the rash of roseola may be confused with a drug rash.

☆ IT IS COMMON FOR

  · children between six months and two years to break out in a rash after a few days of a high fever.

☞ SEE YOUR PEDIATRICIAN IF

  · your child is not perfectly well by the time the rash breaks out.

  · a rash appears at the same time as the fever.

20 | KAWASAKI DISEASE

Named after a Japanese doctor, not a motorcycle, this recently identified disease is serious because 10 to 20 percent of the children who come down with it can develop problems in their coronary arteries.

Along with at least five days of high fever and swollen glands, the diagnosis of Kawasaki disease includes changes in the eyes, mouth and the skin:

The whites of the eyes have enlarged and easily visible blood vessels most prominent around the iris (the colored part of the eye). This may occur early in the course of the illness and be gone by the time other signs appear. In contrast to everyday conjunctivitis or pinkeye—when there is discharge and tearing, and the whites of the eyes become a uniform pink or red which spreads from the outside inward—Kawasaki disease features no discharge. Also, you can still see the white of the eye between the enlarged blood vessels, and redness spreads outward from the iris.

Around the mouth, the lips are bright red, cracked, and crusted, and there is redness of the mouth and throat and/or swelling of the bumps on the surface of the tongue that make it look like a strawberry.

The skin breaks out in a rash that looks like scarlet fever or one that is made up of scattered red spots like erythema multiforme. The rash is most prominent over large joints like the knees and elbows, whereas in scarlet fever it is most prominent in the groin, armpits, neck, and the fold in front of the elbow.

The hands and feet swell, a redness of the palms and soles appears that stops abruptly at the wrists and ankles, and/or there is peeling of the tips of the fingers and toes by seven to ten days after the illness began.

Nobody is sure what causes Kawasaki disease, but the bulk of evidence suggests that it is a response to some unidentified infection.

Current treatment involves intravenous gamma

globulin and aspirin as well as consultation with a pediatric cardiologist to assess the possibility of heart damage. A child suspected of having Kawasaki disease is sometimes hospitalized, but not always.

☞ SEE YOUR PEDIATRICIAN *IMMEDIATELY* IF

• there is a chance your child may have Kawasaki disease. Early treatment can reduce the risk of heart disease.

| 21 | LYME DISEASE (ERYTHEMA |
| | CHRONICUM MIGRANS) |

Lyme disease was named after the town of Lyme, Connecticut, where it was first described in 1977. It is transmitted by the bite of an infected deer tick and causes flulike symptoms one to four weeks later which can be followed by attacks of joint pains, particularly in the knees, as well as heart and nervous system problems.

Because Lyme disease can have many complications including heart and eye problems, it is important to diagnose it early and treat it with antibiotics. Lyme disease, however, is difficult to diagnose, because not every case has a clear history of a tick bite followed by the characteristic rash. Also, since children are often bitten in the scalp, the rash may be missed because it is covered by hair.

Around the tick bite, an expanding ring gradually enlarges and fades. Originally a clear-cut ring, it may eventually develop wavy edges as it fades in the middle. It may be circular, triangular, or oval. The ring also may be an expanding flat red circle with varying intensities of redness inside.

The rash of Lyme disease may resemble ringworm at first, especially if the bite in the center is not obvious, but ringworm takes days or weeks to change appearance, while the rash of Lyme disease changes over a few days.

☞ SEE YOUR PEDIATRICIAN **IMMEDIATELY** IF

- there is a chance your child has Lyme disease.

| 22 | MEASLES (RUBEOLA, TEN-DAY MEASLES, BIG MEASLES) |

Parents often call me thinking their child has measles when they really have roseola, scarlet fever, or a viral rash. Besides having a pinpoint rash that runs together starting on the face and spreading quickly to the rest of the body, children with measles are really sick, with a high fever, a brassy or barking cough, a clear runny nose, and red eyes.

A trademark of measles is "Koplik spots," small red spots with white centers scattered on the membrane lining the inside of the mouth, but these are only present in the first few days.

The complications of measles—pneumonia and encephalitis—while uncommon, can be serious and there is no treatment for the disease once it starts. You can only try to make a child more comfortable and hope that it will end without permanent damage or death. Immunization is the most important measure you can take to prevent the disease, so be sure your child has all the required measles vaccinations.

☞ SEE YOUR PEDIATRICIAN FOR

- confirmation of the diagnosis, information about how to spot potential complications, and suggestions for making your child more comfortable.

| 23 | MOLES |

Ninety-nine percent of all newborns have no moles at birth, but the vast majority of people will develop at least one during the first thirty years of life. White people average fifteen to forty moles by adulthood, blacks only two.

Only 0.1 percent of malignant melanomas arise from moles that appeared during childhood, but moles which are present right around the time of birth are a different story. Depending on which study you read, current statistics are that somewhere between 2 and 14 percent of these moles become malignant. Any mole that arises in the first fourteen days of life should be followed closely by a dermatologist and perhaps removed before puberty.

Normal moles are tan, brown, or blue-black; have a regular border; are less than five millimeters in diameter; and darken with age. If a mole has several different colors or shades within it, is larger across than a pencil eraser, and/or has irregular borders and a variable surface, it is of more concern. These worrisome moles do not appear until late childhood and are mostly on the back. They should be evaluated by a dermatologist because they do have a slightly increased risk of becoming malignant, although probably more than 50 percent of all white people have at least one of these *dysplastic* moles.

♥ IT IS NORMAL FOR
- children to develop moles as they get older.

☞ SEE YOUR PEDIATRICIAN IF
- a mole is present at birth or appears in the first fourteen days of life.
- any mole is irregular in shape, color, or surface.

| 24 | MOLLUSCUM CONTAGIOSUM |

Caused by a virus related to chicken pox but looking more like warts, molluscum begins as tiny, firm, pearly white or flesh-colored bumps with a tiny pit in the center. Most common between ages three and twelve, they are caught from other children either by direct skin contact or from bathing or swimming together.

They may crop up anywhere on the body including the genitals, but tend to appear most frequently on the trunk, groin, armpit, and neck.

Sometimes molluscum itches a little, and scratching may redden the skin surrounding the bumps, but they do not normally cause any irritation.

The bumps of molluscum may last from 2 weeks to 1½ years. Although they do no harm and cause only minimal if any discomfort, they are sometimes cosmetically troublesome and can become infected if children scratch or pick at them, in which case a dermatologist can remove them.

☞ SEE YOUR PEDIATRICIAN FOR

- confirmation of the diagnosis.
- referral to a pediatric dermatologist for removal if the molluscum bumps are numerous or disfiguring.

| 25 | PETECHIAE |

Tiny bright red dots under the skin which do not blanch when you press on them are caused by microscopic bleeding from the smallest blood vessels, the capillaries. Any such bleeding is abnormal, but the cause may not be serious.

Viral infections cause petechiae by damaging the capillaries or by decreasing platelets, microscopic material in the bloodstream that stops bleeding when we get a minor cut.

Sneezing, coughing, or vomiting can bring showers of petechiae to the face. If there are none anywhere else and your child is otherwise well, there is no cause for alarm. Babies may have facial petechiae at birth because of the stresses and strains of going through the birth canal. In fact, even mothers can develop them from pushing during labor.

Tight clothing that constricts an arm or leg in an infant can cause petechiae to form downstream from the constriction; for example, a tight sleeve can cause petechiae on the lower arm or hand. Your child should still be checked to make sure the platelet count is normal, but there may be nothing wrong.

Idiopathic thrombocytopenia (ITP) causes low levels of platelets in a child who seems otherwise perfectly healthy. Although it usually clears up without any treatment, it may require strong medication or even hospitalization in severe cases if the platelet count is dangerously low.

One of the most worrisome possibilities that can cause petechiae is *meningococcemia,* a bacterial infection that can be rapidly fatal.

If you notice pinpoint bleeding under the skin along with fever, or your child is acting sick, go to your pediatrician's office or an emergency room immediately.

The possibility of serious infection is minimal, however, if the petechiae are only on the face and shoulders.

☎ CALL YOUR PEDIATRICIAN FOR
- any evidence of petechiae.

☞ GO TO YOUR PEDIATRICIAN OR AN EMERGENCY ROOM *IMMEDIATELY* IF
- you see petechiae and your child is acting sick, or has a fever.
- the spots are all over your child's body.
- the spots are large and some areas look like bruises.

| 26 | PITYRIASIS ROSEA |

Pityriasis is sometimes preceded by signs of a mild viral infection—sore throat, slight fever, headache and tiredness—but usually there is no preceding illness. Although it may be caused by a virus, it does not spread from one child to another but breaks out only in one child in a group or family. It is more common in children who are preteen to teenagers, although it can erupt in younger children, also.

The first sign is a large ring with scaly, red edges somewhere on the trunk or back, occasionally on the face. This "herald patch" may either not appear at all or go unnoticed and fade before the rest of the rash appears. The herald patch looks a lot like ringworm, with which it might be confused.

Within one to thirty days, however, the diagnosis will become clear. Small, red, scaly, oval-shaped patches appear mostly on the trunk, the arms and legs, the neck, and sometimes the face. In black children, these patches may not be so prominent on the trunk but more apparent on the upper arms, legs, and neck. The spots on the trunk are oriented outward and downward from the center of the child's back like the branches of a Christmas tree. (See illustration, page 180.)

Itching is not usually a problem, but may occur when your child is sweating or becomes warm after going to bed.

The rash lasts four to eight weeks, and there is no treatment.

☞ SEE YOUR PEDIATRICIAN FOR
 • confirmation of the diagnosis.

☎ CALL YOUR PEDIATRICIAN FOR
 • suggestions to relieve itching.

| 27 | PSORIASIS |

Psoriasis, almost never present in infants, strikes the scalp, the crease of the buttocks, the tops of the knees, the outside of the elbows, and/or the genital area. Well-

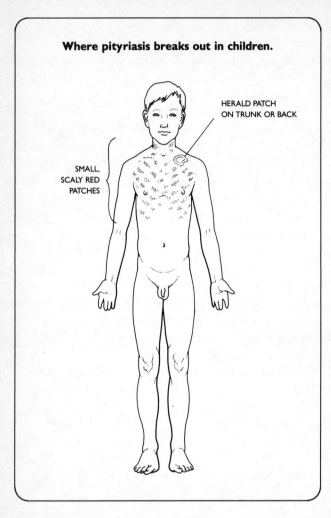

Where pityriasis breaks out in children.

HERALD PATCH
ON TRUNK OR BACK

SMALL,
SCALY RED
PATCHES

demarcated, raised, red areas develop a shiny silvery scale on top.

Psoriasis itches little if at all, but many children with psoriasis develop tiny pits in their nails, crumbly nails, or separation of the nail from the nailbed. Psoriasis may continue into adulthood, in contrast to eczema, which almost always clears up before puberty. It is also much less common than eczema and has little or no relation to a history of allergy in the family, but there is often a history of psoriasis in the family.

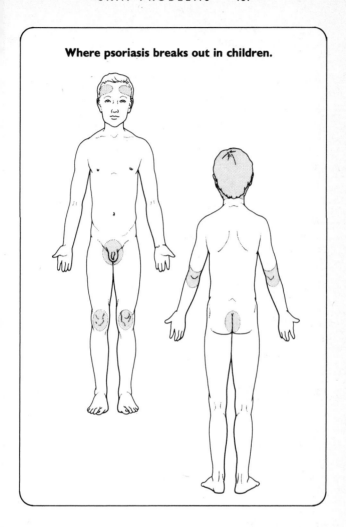

Where psoriasis breaks out in children.

Psoriasis can be confused with other rashes such as pityriasis rosea or eczema, so you should see your pediatrician to confirm the diagnosis. Usually pediatricians refer children with psoriasis to a dermatologist.

⊗ IT IS **NOT** COMMON FOR

- children to develop psoriasis.

☞ SEE YOUR PEDIATRICIAN FOR

- diagnosis, treatment, and possible referral.

28 | RINGWORM

There is no real worm in ringworm, which is really a fungus or yeast infection. It carries that name because it usually forms a ring—one or several round, red, slightly raised rings with scaling edges and clearing in the center. It can appear on any part of the body including the scalp, where it causes a round area of hair loss as well as a scaly rash.

The rings grow slowly and last a long time. It is easy to confuse this with the herald patch of pityriasis rosea, and sometimes eczema or psoriasis can form similar rings. An uncommon rash called *granuloma annulare* is also quite similar to ringworm.

If your pediatrician has trouble diagnosing this, it may be necessary to take a scraping from the edge of the circle to identify the fungus under the microscope or grow it in culture.

Ringworm is more common in hot, humid climates and in children who live in crowded conditions, but it can appear in any child. It can be transmitted from a dog or cat, from another child, or from soil in the ground.

Some over-the-counter medications such as Micatin work well. If they do not, your pediatrician can prescribe a stronger preparation either to apply to the skin or take internally.

☞ SEE YOUR PEDIATRICIAN IF

- you need to confirm the diagnosis of ringworm.
- the prescribed treatment does not seem to be effective after two weeks.

29 | SCABIES

The mite that causes scabies, a microscopic insect too small to be seen with the naked eye, burrows under the skin of the abdomen, the backs of the hands and tops of the feet, the wrists and palms, and especially the webs of skin between the fingers and toes. The head and neck are almost never involved in children, but can be in infants. Scattered small dry bumps sometimes have a linear burrow on one end if you look carefully.

Itching is common and may begin a day or two before the rash breaks out. It is most severe at night. Infants who are too young to scratch rub their hands and feet together. Scratching may lead to impetigo, which can complicate the picture. Sometimes it is hard to tell the difference between the crusty, dry skin of eczema or swimmer's itch and an early case of scabies.

Although it is possible to catch scabies from animals, it is most often transmitted person to person. Itching does not begin for three days to a month after a person is infected, so children can infect others before it is apparent that they are infected.

If your child has scabies, your pediatrician may recommend treating the entire family. Applying a special cream or lotion to the skin for several hours cures the vast majority of cases. Even if the insect is effectively killed, itching may persist for several weeks after treatment.

Usually people have scabies only once, which leads doctors to believe that we form antibodies and become immune to it after the first episode.

The mite cannot live more than two to four days away from human skin. Normal laundering and dry cleaning of clothes and bed linens are all that is necessary, and there will be no live mites on fabrics if they have not been in contact with human skin for a few days.

☆ IT IS COMMON FOR

- children to have scabies.

☞ SEE YOUR PEDIATRICIAN IF

- you need to confirm the diagnosis and get a prescription to treat it.

- scratching causes impetigo.
- simple treatment does not clear it up in one to two weeks.

| 30 | SCARLET FEVER (SCARLATINA) |

Scarlet fever can occur at almost any age but is most common in children between two and ten. It is caused by infection with the strep germ, but sometimes a staph infection can cause the same rash. Some children are not very sick with it while others are.

The usual source is a strep throat, but an infection anywhere—even a vaginal strep infection—may be the culprit.

The rash starts on the face and travels down the body. The spots concentrate on the folds of the skin like those of the groin, neck, armpit, and elbow. Sometimes the rash is so severe that capillaries break and small bleeding points (petechiae) appear in skin folds. The palms of the hands and soles of the feet are not involved.

The rash of toxic shock (see page 187) can mimic scarlet fever, but toxic shock usually has associated diarrhea, faintness, and vomiting.

Swollen glands are common if the infection is in the throat.

A week or two after the infection begins, the tips of the fingers and toes may peel.

Prompt treatment with an antibiotic may reduce the risk of complications such as rheumatic fever and kidney inflammation.

☞ SEE YOUR PEDIATRICIAN IF

- you suspect scarlet fever.

☞ SEE YOUR PEDIATRICIAN OR GO TO AN EMERGENCY ROOM *IMMEDIATELY* IF

- your child is acting sick or has a high fever.

• a scarlet fever rash is associated with vomiting, diarrhea, fainting, or inability to sit up or stand.

31 | SHOE DERMATITIS

It is understandable to think that your child's red, cracking foot rash is athlete's foot, but it probably is not. The truth is that athlete's foot is uncommon before puberty. The culprit is probably your child's shoes.

Athlete's foot causes a rash and cracking between the toes, whereas a shoe reaction breaks out on the top and bottom of the foot with no rash between the toes.

This has nothing to do with how expensive or cheap the shoes were, but rather that your child's feet are enclosed in a warm, moist environment in which chemicals from adhesives, leather, or plastic can sensitize the skin.

Letting your child go barefoot as much as possible, changing to dry socks at regular intervals, and sometimes using a cortisone cream usually solves the problem.

☆ IT IS COMMON FOR
• children to develop a rash from wearing shoes.

☎ CALL YOUR PEDIATRICIAN IF
• you cannot clear it up with simple measures.
• there is cracking, bleeding, pain, and itching between the toes—signs of athlete's foot.

32 | STRAWBERRY MARKS

Although many people call these birthmarks, they are not usually present at birth but arise sometime later. Only 2.5 percent of all babies have strawberry marks when they are born, but by one year 10 to 12 percent of all white infants have one or more.

Soft, bright, cherry red, bumpy-surfaced marks appear anywhere on the body, although the majority are on the head and trunk. They may be tiny or enormous. During the first six months of life they enlarge, from six to ten months growth slows down, and by twelve months they are as large as they will ever get. By age five, half are gone, and by age nine, all but 10 percent have disappeared. In the process they go from bright red to a dull purple with white or gray areas in the center and then completely disappear.

Twenty percent of all strawberry marks leave behind them light areas of skin, scarring, or a permanent collection of little blood vessels visible underneath the skin.

If a strawberry mark occurs on the lower back, especially if it spans the middle, there may be a spinal cord problem underneath.

Strawberry marks have nothing to do with anything a mother did or felt during pregnancy. Although it is uncommon to need treatment for them, strawberry marks which interfere with normal function (such as one that prevents a child from seeing out of one eye) can be treated with a special laser to shrink them.

♥ IT IS NORMAL FOR
• babies to develop strawberry marks during the first year of life.

☎ CALL IT TO YOUR PEDIATRICIAN'S ATTENTION IF
• the mark is on the lower back, especially if it crosses the middle.
• there are multiple marks all over (rarely, this can be a sign of internal problems).

| 33 | SWIMMER'S ITCH, SEABATHER'S ERUPTION |

Children may develop a rash from infection with parasites that live in lakes or oceans. After swimming in fresh water, itchy bumps arise in areas *not* covered by a bathing suit, and in salt water, the bumps arise in areas *underneath* the bathing suit. The rash may persist for two weeks, and can be quite itchy.

There is no treatment necessary except to control the itching, because it goes away by itself.

A similar rash may appear after soaking in a hot tub. This one is caused by a bacteria that thrives in warm water. It also does not need any treatment.

All these rashes can be confused with scabies and other kinds of rashes, so you must see your pediatrician to confirm the diagnosis.

☞ SEE YOUR PEDIATRICIAN IF

- a rash appears after swimming.

| 34 | TOXIC SHOCK |

This life-threatening syndrome received a lot of publicity because of its association with tampons, but actually it can occur in children of any age and in both sexes. It is caused by a poison produced by a bacterial infection. In the case of tampons, the infection is in the vagina, but infection anywhere in the body can cause it.

The rash of toxic shock might look just like the rash of scarlet fever, with tiny spots coalescing into a diffuse redness most pronounced in the folds of the armpits, the groin, and the neck. Children with toxic shock may have a fever at the beginning of the illness, just like those with scarlet fever. The differences are that vomiting and diarrhea frequently precede the onset of the rash in toxic shock, the hands and feet may swell, and children become faint and pale or even pass out when upright—all of which do not usually occur with scarlet fever.

The rash of toxic shock also resembles Kawasaki disease, but the fever in toxic shock lasts only two or three days, versus a week or more with Kawasaki, and

diarrhea, vomiting, and prostration are more pronounced with toxic shock. Rapid treatment in the hospital is essential because as many as 3 percent of children
with toxic shock may die.

☞ SEE YOUR PEDIATRICIAN OR GO TO AN EMERGENCY
ROOM IF

• your child has a scarlet fever–type rash and is
acting very sick, seems excessively tired, is vomiting
and/or has diarrhea, or cannot sit or stand up.

| 35 | VIRAL RASH (SEE "DRUG RASH," PAGE 159).

| 36 | WARTS

Warts are caused by a virus, not by handling toads.
Although they can appear anywhere, in children they
are most common on the hands, and often involve the
skin around the base of the fingernails. They may be flat
or raised, tiny or huge.

Unless the wart is on an area that has regular pressure
such as the sole of the foot or a finger involved with
writing, warts are mostly a cosmetic nuisance.

If you do nothing, most warts will go away in a year
or two. Those that are painful or disfiguring can be
removed. If the wart is not on the face or the sole of
the foot, try over-the-counter wart removers. They are
inexpensive, painless, and many times that is all that is
necessary.

For facial or plantar warts (on the sole of the foot),
or if simple measures do not work in a few weeks, see
your pediatrician or a dermatologist for advice or removal. However, a dermatologist whom I respect has
three rules about warts:

1. They come back a lot.
2. They come back a lot.
3. They come back a lot.

♥ IT IS NORMAL FOR
- children to have warts here and there.

⊗ IT IS **NOT** NORMAL FOR
- newborns to have warts.
- children to have warts around the anus or genital area.

☞ SEE YOUR PEDIATRICIAN OR ASK FOR A REFERRAL FOR
- warts on the sole of the foot or on the face.
- warts that do not respond to simple measures.
- examination of what appears to be a wart in an infant (this may be something else).
- warts around the anus or genitals.

Bones &

Joints

| I | GENERAL PRINCIPLES |

A. Not Moving a Limb, With or Without an Injury

It takes quite a lot of pain to keep a child from running or playing. Although copious tears may flow at the time of an injury, a kiss on the booboo and a short rest are usually all your child needs before she takes off again. Anytime your child complains of persistent pain in the same place or refuses to use an arm or leg, suspect a broken bone or other significant problem.

B. How to Know If a Bone Is Broken

One of my teachers in medical school said that children's bones heal as long as both ends are in the same room, and generally that is true. The unique problem for children is that their bones are still growing. Even a minor injury that involves the growth center can lead to abnormalities later, so have any suspicious, persistent pain examined.

See A., "Is It Broken?" pages 220–21, for more details.

⊗ IT IS **NOT** NORMAL FOR

- children to refuse to move an arm or leg.

☞ SEE YOUR PEDIATRICIAN IF

- at anytime your child complains of persistent pain and refuses to move a body part.

| 2 | THE ARMS |

A. Holding the Arm Slightly Bent and Not Moving; Nursemaid's Elbow; Dislocated Radial Head

You are crossing the street with your recalcitrant preschooler and she suddenly decides to sit down or to run the other way. Your natural response is to pull firmly on the hand you are holding. This can cause a fleeting displacement of one of the bones in the elbow. The bone actually returns to a normal position, but a ligament is trapped between the bones. This can also happen when children are flung around by their arms when they play or if they fall on an arm in just the wrong way.

The injury itself does not usually hurt much at the time, but afterward your child will be reluctant to move the arm, holding it slightly bent with the palm of the hand facing downward and will not let anyone touch the elbow.

There is a simple maneuver that your pediatrician can do to replace everything where it should be. If you go to an emergency room, your child is more likely to have an x-ray which may not be necessary, so call your pediatrician first.

On rare occasions, an underlying problem such as a bone defect becomes obvious only after an arm is injured. If the arm cannot be easily relocated or pain persists, or if there are any other signs such as fever, swelling, or redness, further tests will be necessary.

☆ IT IS COMMON FOR

· preschool-aged children to suffer a minor dislocation in the elbow.

☞ SEE YOUR PEDIATRICIAN FOR

· proper diagnosis and treatment to replace the arm into its normal position.

☞ SEE YOUR PEDIATRICIAN *IMMEDIATELY* IF

· there are any other signs of illness.

B. Wrist Pain After a Fall

Children's bones are like green twigs. They can bend and break without actually snapping apart. Not infequently, a fall that seems relatively minor may produce persistent pain in the wrist.

Children do not often "sprain" their ankles or wrists as adults do, so pain that endures beyond the immediate period after the injury is likely due to a *greenstick* fracture at the end of the radius (the large bone of the forearm) near the wrist. One of my office nurses was mortified when she brought her daughter in several days after she fell because she kept complaining of a sore wrist and it turned out that her radius was broken. The girl's fracture healed nicely, but I don't think my nurse has gotten over the feeling of being a negligent mother.

⊗ IT IS *NOT* NORMAL FOR

· children to have persistent pain in the wrist after a fall.

☞ SEE YOUR PEDIATRICIAN IF

· there is any persistent pain.

| 3 | THE LEGS |

A. Bowlegs

A mild bowlegged curve is normal up to age two, after which the legs straighten out by themselves. In some children, walking early (under age one), obesity, or walking with feet abnormally far apart may cause an imbalance in the pressures and stresses on growing knees, which may in turn lead to an *increase* in bowing between ages two and four. The vast majority of these children require no treatment for this.

Only in rare instances is surgery necessary. There are no special shoes that can speed up the natural process of straightening out.

♥ IT IS NORMAL FOR

· children to be a little bowlegged up to age two and even beyond.

☞ SEE YOUR PEDIATRICIAN IF

· a curve in the legs seems to be increasing rather than decreasing by age four.

B. Knock-Knees

After the normal bowleggedness of infancy straightens out by age three or four, children may become slightly knock-kneed. It is especially obvious in slender children who have what I call "flamingo legs." This pretty nearly always corrects itself by age ten to eleven in girls and twelve to thirteen in boys.

Having the shoemaker put wedges in shoes and other treatments you may have heard about are a waste of time and money. If knock-knees are severe and do not correct by themselves, bone surgery is the only treatment that can correct them.

♥ IT IS NORMAL FOR

- children to be knock-kneed until just before puberty.

☞ SEE YOUR PEDIATRICIAN IF

- the deformity is severe, interferes with walking or running, and is not improved by ten to eleven in girls, twelve to thirteen in boys.

C. Leg Pains

i. Growing Pains

I remember many nights as a child waking up with crampy pain in my thighs and calves. My mother would rub them or put me in a hot bath, and they would subside in a few minutes.

About 90 percent of children's complaints about pain in the legs or calves are due to these "growing pains." One out of ten children between ages three and ten suffer from these intermittent muscular aches. They are most troublesome in the evening or just after bedtime and disappear during the day. They never make children limp, but they are often severe enough to awaken children from sleep and even cry with the pain.

Nobody knows what causes them. Theories ranging from rheumatic fever to psychological pain have been suggested and tested over the years, and none of them hold water. The only thing we know for sure is what they are *not*. They are not serious or disabling.

Massage, heat (a hot water bottle or a warm rub), reassurance, a mild pain reliever, and time are about all that is necessary to treat them. A program of stretching exercises helps control pains for some children.

The probability of anything serious is minuscule. Nevertheless, if pains keep recurring over several years, it is a good idea to have your pediatrician check your child every six to twelve months to be sure there isn't something else brewing.

♥ IT IS NORMAL FOR

- children between ages three and ten to have nighttime cramps in the muscles of the thighs and calves.

☎ CALL YOUR PEDIATRICIAN IF

- the pain is present during the day.
- your child limps.
- pains persist after age twelve.
- pain seems to be in a joint, not in a muscle.
- there is any redness or tenderness where it hurts.
- there is fever along with pain.

ii. Shin Splints

Pain along the inner or outer surface of the lower leg can come from muscle pain after unaccustomed physical activity such as resuming track after laying off all winter, or a long walk around Disney World. I used to get them all the time as an intern, running through the miles of corridors at UCLA Hospital.

The pain of shin splints decreases with rest and periodic ice packs. Vigorous activity should be resumed gradually to avoid a recurrence.

If there is pain or tenderness on the bony bump just below the knee, this may be *Osgood Schlatter's disease.* Inflammation of this protrusion is caused by vigorous activity, and happens more commonly in children close to or going through adolescence, and is treated the same as shin splints.

If what appears to be shin splints really involves a single, highly tender spot on the shin bone, you may be dealing with a stress fracture (see the next section).

♥ IT IS NORMAL FOR

- children to suffer from shin splints after vigorous, especially unaccustomed, activity.

☞ CALL YOUR PEDIATRICIAN IF

- pain does not improve with rest.
- there is redness or swelling in the area of tenderness.

- one particular spot hurts rather than the whole side of the shin.

iii. Stress Fractures

Regular, strenuous physical activity that causes repeated minor trauma to the legs—track, gymnastics, or dancing, for example—can produce a tiny break on the surface of a bone in the lower leg that can be quite painful. You may be able to locate the site of the fracture by pressing on one point.

Stress fractures do not show up right away on an x-ray, so if your pediatrician suspects one but an x-ray is normal, your child may have to undergo a bone scan. This can pinpoint a stress fracture before it shows up on an x-ray.

Unlike other small fractures in children which heal quickly, these may take several weeks to heal. Although the bone is not out of line and does not need to be "set," a walking cast may bring welcome relief.

☆ IT IS COMMON FOR

- children who participate actively in sports to suffer from stress fractures.

☞ SEE YOUR PEDIATRICIAN IF

- persistent pain is most severe at one point on a bone.

D. Snapping, Clicking, or Popping Knee

If you notice that your infant's leg pops or clicks when you change diapers, there may be a problem in the hip joint. Although most of the time this is merely due to a tendon snapping as it passes over a joint, it could be due to a shallow hip socket. Bring it to your pediatrician's attention at the next checkup.

Between ages six and eight some children complain of a snapping or popping knee that does not hurt but may feel like it is "giving way" or "catching." You may detect a "clunk" as your child straightens the leg.

This can be caused by abnormal cartilage in the knee or by a tendon that snaps as it travels over a bone.

Most of the time no treatment is necessary. However, if your child is athletic and vigorously participates in sports such as football, basketball, or tennis in which the knee has a good chance to be injured, consult an orthopedic surgeon about the advisability of continued participation.

⊖ IT IS NOT NECESSARILY A PROBLEM

- when a child has a snapping or popping knee.

☞ SEE YOUR PEDIATRICIAN IF

- your infant's knee or leg snaps when you change his diapers.
- there is pain associated with the "pop" or your child has fallen when the knee "gives."
- your child wants to play an active, contact sport that could risk damage to the knee.

---

4 | THE FEET

A. Pigeon Toes

Feet that turn in can be caused by a problem in the feet, the lower leg, or the hip.

Since most in-toeing is the result of minor problems that clear up by themselves over time, be wary of shoe sellers who try to sell you "corrective shoes" without consulting your pediatrician.

Feet: Some babies are born with an inward curve to one or both feet. Although this is thought to be caused by the way the baby was folded up inside the uterus, it also tends to run in families. About 85 percent of the time, this curve will clear up on its own by the age of one year.

If the curve is severe or does not seem to be correcting on its own, your pediatrician may refer you to an orthopedist for casts or special shoes. If the foot does not straighten out by the time your child walks, it will be difficult to find shoes that fit.

Many toddlers appear to be pigeon-toed because of the monkeylike grasp they have with their toes when they are just learning to walk. If the foot is straight at rest, there is no need to do anything about this. Once your child is an experienced walker, it will go away.

Lower leg: An inward twist of the lower leg between the knee and ankle is called *tibial torsion.* Quite common in children, it is rarely severe enough to cause tripping, and in 99 out of 100 cases the twist resolves on its own as a child grows.

If it is severe, your pediatrician will refer you to an orthopedist, who may prescribe a night splint. This contraption is used during sleep to hold the feet outward in shoes attached to a metal bar. It is only effective, however, if used in children too young to figure out how to take the shoes off and use the whole apparatus as a missile. It does not help at all after age three.

The hip: An inward rotation of the thigh at the hip joint can twist the whole leg inward. Children with this problem have a tendency to sit in a "w" position because that is most comfortable. It helps to encourage sitting tailor fashion so that the hips are rotated outward instead.

However, because this position is not as comfortable, it is usually difficult to make children sit that way habitually.

In only 1 percent of all children does this problem not correct on its own between the ages of five and ten. In the rare cases that do not, surgery may be necessary to prevent hip and knee problems later in life.

(child in a tailor position)

How children who toe in sit.

(child in a "w" position)

A better way to sit.

♥ IT IS NORMAL FOR

· children to appear to be pigeon-toed for the first few years they walk.

☞ CALL YOUR PEDIATRICIAN IF

· in-toeing is so severe it is causing your child to trip.

· you notice an inward curve to your infant's foot.

- pigeon toes do not clear up by age ten.
- in-turning involves only one foot or leg.

B. Toes Turning Out (Walking like a Duck)

Keeping the feet turned outward is actually beneficial for stability when walking. It is virtually unheard of that anything needs to be done about toeing out and it corrects itself as your child grows. Dancers and skaters, in fact, do better if they have a "natural turnout"!

♥ IT IS NORMAL FOR

- children to turn their feet outward when they walk.

C. Flat Feet

Children under five *look* as though they have flat feet because there is a pad of fat underneath the arch of the foot. Once this pad disappears, you will see a normal arch.

If your child over five looks as though the feet are still flat, there are two possible causes which you can diagnose yourself by having your child stand on tiptoe.

The most common is the so-called *flexible* flat foot. When your child stands on tiptoe, there is an obvious arch, but when standing flat on the floor, the heel rolls inward a little and there is no obvious arch. The major problem with this type of flat foot is that shoes wear out inordinately quickly at the inside and back of the heels.

If there is no pain in the feet, you need not do anything. A wedge in the heel will not correct the problem in the foot but will allow shoes to last a little longer. If your child complains of foot pain after standing, walking, or running, see your pediatrician or an orthopedist familiar with children. Do *not* ask a salesperson in a shoe store for advice; you may be sold an unnecessarily expensive pair of shoes.

A rigid flat foot does not form an arch when your child stands on tiptoe. This type of flatness is much less common than the flexible kind, and is caused by an abnormal fusion between two bones of the foot. It is almost always painful—if not now, then later in life. Your pediatrician will refer you to a pediatric orthopedist for pain relief and possible surgery when your child is older.

♥ IT IS NORMAL FOR
- children's feet to appear to be flat until age five.

☞ SEE YOUR PEDIATRICIAN FOR
- feet that hurt.
- flat feet that do not form an arch when your child stands on tiptoe.

D. Overlapping Toes

Many children are born with one toe overlapping another, most commonly the second and third toes. Often someone in the family has had overlapping toes also.

Under the age of one, no treatment is necessary because most children will correct this as they grow and walk.

If you have a problem finding shoes that fit because of the overlapping toes, your pediatrician can show you how to tape them into a better position until they correct themselves. Surgery is not usually considered until after age three, and it can be put off until adolescence if there is no pain and shoes fit well enough.

☆ IT IS COMMON FOR
- children to have overlapping toes on both feet.

☞ BRING IT TO YOUR PEDIATRICIAN'S ATTENTION IF
- fitting shoes is difficult.
- your child has pain.
- the toes become sore from rubbing.

| 5 | WALKING |

A. Refusal to Walk in a Child Who Has Already Learned to Walk

Any child who is able to walk but refuses to must be seen by a pediatrician promptly. There may be nothing more than a splinter in a foot, but the possibility exists that this is an early sign of a number of problems—for example, an infection in a bone or joint, rheumatoid arthritis, or *discitis,* a smoldering infection in the back.

⊗ IT IS **NOT** NORMAL FOR
- children to refuse to walk.

☞ SEE YOUR PEDIATRICIAN IF
- your child is able to walk but refuses to do so.

B. Limping

One of the mothers in my practice was relieved but slightly embarrassed when she brought her child in for a troublesome limp and it turned out that the child's shoe was too tight on one foot. Check to see if your child limps the same with and without shoes and inspect the bottom of the foot and toes carefully. Limping can sometimes be due to something as simple as a nail in the bottom of a shoe.

Children who received an immunization in a thigh may have pain and limp for a day or two afterward. Usually there is a tender swelling at the place where the shot went in.

If your child limps after an injury to the foot or ankle, rest, elevate, and ice the injured area and wait awhile to see if it gets better.

Children who limp and complain of pain in the thigh or the knee may actually have a problem in the hip. In fact, between 10 and 20 percent of all complaints about knee pain in children come from the hip. A branch of a nerve going to the knee passes over the hip joint, and irritation or inflammation in the hip irritates the nerve, sending a signal that the body mistakes as coming from the knee.

The most common hip problem in young children is *synovitis,* inflammation of the membranes surrounding the hip joint caused by minor injury or a viral infection. Limping may start gradually at first, followed by complaints of pain a little later. Bed rest for a day or two usually brings prompt improvement, although synovitis does not go away completely for one to three weeks.

Hip pain in older children—between ages three and twelve, with a peak incidence at age six, can result from *Legge-Perthe's disease,* a problem with circulation to the top of the thigh bone. In contrast to synovitis, Legge-Perthe's may require several years and specialized treatment to heal.

Lyme disease, an infection transmitted by the bite of a specific tick, can cause joint pain, most commonly in the knee, two to three weeks after the bite. Usually the joints are not swollen, hot, or red, and a limp may be the first sign that your child has knee pain. Lyme disease is sometimes a difficult diagnosis for a doctor to make, because evidence of a tick bite and the characteristic rash are not always apparent.

Rheumatic fever is still uncommon but on the rise. A rash and fever accompanied by joint pain, usually the elbows and knees, following a strep infection may cause your child to limp.

About 200,000 children in the United States develop some form of *juvenile rheumatoid arthritis* during childhood. Usually there is a fever and obvious joint swelling, but sometimes this can start as a limp from a painful knee.

The most serious possibility is that pain and limping could be caused by infection in a joint, or *septic arthritis,* or an infection deep inside a bone—*osteomyelitis.* By the time redness, swelling, and fever have made the diagnosis apparent, some destruction of the bone or joint may already have occurred. Therefore, pediatricians treat undiagnosed joint problems as serious until proven otherwise. Your pediatrician may order blood tests, x-rays, and possibly a bone scan. If those tests are normal, you and your pediatrician will probably continue to watch your child closely for a few days.

⊗ IT IS **NOT** NORMAL FOR

- children to limp, although it does not always mean that there is a serious problem.

☞ SEE YOUR PEDIATRICIAN IF

- any limp lasts more than a day or two.
- your child complains of joint pain that comes and goes.

☞ SEE YOUR PEDIATRICIAN **IMMEDIATELY** IF

- a limp is associated with fever, rash, swollen joints, or any other sign of illness.

C. Toe Walking

Many children walk on their toes for a few months after they first learn to walk. In one third of these cases, there is a family history of the same behavior. Most of the time, your child will start walking with the feet flat on the ground in a short time.

Under the age of one, there is no need to worry. After that, make sure your child is able to stand still with the feet flat on the ground without any pain. If that is difficult, the heel cord in the back of the ankle may be too tight—the most common reason for abnormal toe walking.

Tight heel cords can stretch with physical therapy and special braces in the shoes. Only one child out of a hundred ever needs surgery to correct this. A tight heel cord on only one side can be due to an event in the brain that happened before birth or a mild form of clubfoot.

Toe walking that starts in a slightly older child—eighteen months to two years—who previously walked with a flat foot, should be checked. This may be a sign of minor neurological damage that was present at birth but took some time to become apparent.

♥ IT IS NORMAL FOR

· children to walk on their toes for a few months after starting to walk.

☞ SEE YOUR PEDIATRICIAN IF

· your child cannot stand with the feet flat.
· only one leg is involved.
· there is a limp along with toe walking.
· your child was previously walking normally but starts to toe-walk later.

---

6 | JOINT SWELLING, WITH OR WITHOUT PAIN

Joint swelling can have many causes—an injury, a bone or joint infection or inflammation, a drug reaction, rheumatic fever, Lyme disease or rheumatoid arthritis are some. A foreign body under the skin or a skin infection near a joint can cause what appears to be joint swelling but is really only a superficial skin problem.

The most serious cause of swelling is a joint infection, or *septic arthritis,* because it can rapidly destroy a normal joint. Septic arthritis can occur at any age but it is most common in children under three. The hip, knee, and elbow are most frequent, but any joint may be involved. I've even had a child who had an infection of the joint between the collarbone and the shoulder.

Although signs of infection are characteristically fever, redness, and tenderness, these may not be evident in the early stages. In fact, by the time these changes are obvious, some joint destruction may have already occurred.

Therefore, see your pediatrician immediately for any swelling in any joint. Septic arthritis must be diagnosed and treated early to minimize complications.

⊗ IT IS **NOT** NORMAL FOR
- children to have swollen joints.

☞ SEE YOUR PEDIATRICIAN **IMMEDIATELY** IF
- there is swelling in any joint.

| 7 | BACK PAIN |

Although there are many benign causes for back pain in adolescents, it is unusual for younger children to have back pain before puberty. While some cases may be due to simple problems such as repetitive trauma from gymnastics or other athletic injuries, back pain in children must always be investigated thoroughly for serious underlying causes.

⊗ IT IS **NOT** NORMAL FOR
- children to have back pain.

☞ SEE YOUR PEDIATRICIAN IF
- your child persistently complains of back pain.

☞ SEE YOUR PEDIATRICIAN **IMMEDIATELY** IF
- any complaints of back pain are accompanied by fever, refusal to walk, blood in the urine, or any other signs of illness.

CHAPTER VIII

Minor Injuries

---

1 | WHO NEEDS A TETANUS SHOT?

The schedule for tetanus shots is:

> 2, 4 and 6 months
> 18 months
> Between ages 4 and 6
> At age fifteen and every ten years thereafter

If your child has a puncture wound, a burn, an animal bite, or a serious cut, check to see when the last tetanus shot was given. If your child is due for one about now, have it within forty-eight hours of the injury.

After age five and for the rest of life, tetanus shots are good for ten years.

---

2 | WHAT TO DO AND WHEN TO CALL
THE DOCTOR FOR:

A. Bee, Wasp, Yellow Jacket, or Hornet Stings

Bees, hornets, yellow jackets, and wasps cause painful stings that hurt immediately but usually stop hurting in an hour or two. Small children are particularly prone to be stung by bumblebees—slow-moving, large, furry bees that nest on the ground.

WHAT TO DO

Rub an ice cube over the sting or run cold water over it for a few minutes to relieve the immediate pain. Do not apply meat tenderizer or other remedies you may have heard about because they can damage a child's tender skin.

If you see a tiny black dot or feel a small, hard point on top of the bite, the stinger is probably still in there. Stingers can be removed either with tweezers or by scraping a plastic credit card or a dull knife across the sting. Avoid squeezing the area of the bite to remove the stinger because you may release more venom.

After you have removed the stinger and applied a cold compress, wait to be sure your child does not have a reaction. Serious allergic reactions happen within a few minutes. Hives, swollen lips or eyes, trouble breathing, paleness, blue color to the lips or skin, or collapse can signal a life-threatening emergency and should be treated promptly by paramedics or in a nearby emergency room. Fortunately, that type of reaction is uncommon.

More commonly, within twenty-four hours a bite on the hand, foot, or face swells dramatically. The amount of swelling far exceeds any discomfort your child seems to have. Soft areas like the back of the hand or the tissue around the eye are especially prone to swell. With this type of local reaction, the swelling will stop sharply at the wrist or ankle. If an infection has set in, swelling and redness are more likely to extend beyond the joint and there will be pain and/or fever as well.

If your child has no fever or pain, merely wait for the swelling to go down. Cool compresses and elevating the swollen part help a little. Antihistamines probably do little if any good. In two or three days the tissue should return to normal.

♥ IT IS NORMAL FOR

• children to have dramatic swelling the day after a sting.

☎ CALL YOUR PEDIATRICIAN IF
· swelling lasts longer than a day or extends beyond the ankle or wrist.
· there are multiple bites, as ten or more stings can make a small child seriously ill.

☎ CALL THE EMERGENCY SQUAD IF
· your child is wheezing, has swollen lips, has difficulty breathing, collapses, or has paleness or blue coloring after an insect sting.

PREVENTING STINGS

▪ Avoid dressing your child in clothing with prints and colors that look like flowers.
▪ Avoid scented soaps and lotions.
▪ Make sure your children wear shoes when playing on grass.
▪ Keep children away from garbage cans and keep cans covered.

B. Animal or Human Bites

Three quarters of a million children are bitten by dogs in the United States every year. And boys are twice as likely as girls to be bitten by dogs, while girls are twice as likely to be bitten by cats. Human bites are less common then animal bites but have increased in recent years because more small children are in group day-care.

Any bite, whether animal or human, can easily become infected, and human bites actually contain more germs than animal bites! The chance of infection is increased if the bite involves crushed tissue as well as broken skin, more than twenty-four hours elapse before medical care is sought, or the bite is on the back of the hand.

WHAT TO DO

If the skin is broken, wash the area with soap and water. A Water Pik helps to squirt water under pressure into all the cracks and crevices. Clear water and soap are just as good as peroxide or antibacterial soaps.

Severe, multiple, or deep bites or those around the head, neck, and hand are particularly prone to serious infection and must be treated for four to five days with antibiotics.

Check when your child's last tetanus shot was given and whether one is due now.

If your child was bitten by a stray or wild animal, either capture the animal alive if you can do it safely or kill it and preserve the head in a plastic bag without touching it to test for rabies.

Rabies is *unlikely* with rats, mice, prairie dogs, hamsters, gerbils, chipmunks, squirrels, rabbits, or hares.

Rabies is *possible* with bites from bats, skunks, raccoons, foxes, coyote, and bobcats.

☎ CALL YOUR PEDIATRICIAN

• to check on your child's tetanus status.
• to check on the possibility of rabies from an animal bite.

☞ SEE YOUR PEDIATRICIAN IF

• there are multiple or deep bites, or if bites were on the head and neck, or on the hand.

C. Tick Bites

Ticks are small brown insects that attach themselves firmly to the skin and swell up with their host's blood, turning a dark or bright red. They lodge most often in the scalp, neck, armpit, and groin. Since they cause no pain or itching, they may remain attached quite a long time before they are discovered. Adult ticks are easy to spot, especially after they fill up with blood, but you have to look carefully for tiny baby ticks.

Ticks should be removed promptly because they can carry a variety of diseases such as Rocky Mountain spotted fever, encephalitis, and Lyme disease. It appears that disease transmission is more likely after a tick has been attached for forty-eight hours, so holding tick inspection every twenty-four hours while on a camping trip or after day hikes is probably adequate.

WHAT TO DO

Using tweezers, grasp the insect firmly as close to the skin as you can, so that the head is gripped rather than just the body. Pull steadily outward without twisting or jerking to avoid leaving the head in the skin.

If the head is left in the skin, try removing it as you would a splinter. If you are unsuccessful, see your pediatrician.

Do not apply a hot match or cigarette to the tick's body or try to crush it. This increases the risk of spreading the germs contained in the tick's body even further.

☞ SEE YOUR PEDIATRICIAN IF

·   you are unsuccessful in removing the entire tick.

·   you see a tick and your child is excessively sleepy or difficult to arouse.

·   a rash, fever, or joint pains develop one to three weeks after a tick bite.

PREVENTING TICK BITES

- Wear insect repellent on all exposed skin.
- Wear long-sleeved shirts and long pants when out in the woods.
- Hold tick inspections at the end of each day you spend in the woods.

D. Minor Burns

All burns in children should be treated as potentially serious, but whether there will be long-lasting or life-threatening problems depends on the degree of burn.

Sunburns and hot water scalds are the most common minor burns in children. Most of these are first-degree burns, which are red, painful, and swollen but heal in five to ten days without scars and with little or no risk of infection.

Second-degree burns cause blistering, severe pain, and swelling. A superficial second-degree burn is one in which the skin underneath the blister is red, and these heal in ten to fourteen days. Deep second-degree burns, which are white underneath the blister, can take up to one month to heal and may scar. They also carry a high risk of infection. Most grease burns have areas of deep second-degree.

Third-degree burns are those caused by direct contact with flames and involve the full thickness of the skin. They are highly prone to infection and may need skin grafts to heal.

WHAT TO DO

For any burn, apply cool compresses or hold the burned part under cold running water immediately. Burning can continue for many seconds to minutes after skin is no longer in contact with the source of heat. Do not use ice; freezing can complicate tissue damage.

Remove any clothing involved in the burn. Hot grease, for example, can keep burning the skin for a long time after it permeates clothing.

Do not apply creams, ointments, or butter, and leave blisters intact until they break by themselves. Just cover the burn with a clean, dry gauze.

☞ SEE YOUR PEDIATRICIAN FOR
- any burn in an infant or child up to age two.
- any burns of the face, hands, feet, or genitals.

· blistering burns that cover more than an inch or two of skin.

AVOIDING BURNS AND SCALDS

- Set your water heater no higher than 120°F.
- Never leave children alone in the tub; they can turn on the hot water tap.
- Turn all pot handles and cords away from the edge of the stove or counter top.
- Avoid tablecloths; children can pull them down along with hot liquids.

E. Sunburn

Not only is a sunburn uncomfortable, but every sunburn in childhood increases the risk of melanoma later in life by 50 percent. It is important, therefore, to prevent sunburn right from birth.

Children can develop burns on overcast or cloudy days, and even if they are kept in the shade. Sunlight can be reflected from water or concrete, even if it does not shine directly onto the child's skin. Sometimes five or ten minutes is enough to cause a burn, which may not reveal itself until after you have gone indoors.

AVOIDING SUNBURN

Apply sunscreen thirty minutes before going out into the sun, every two to four hours, after swimming, and after your child has perspired. And pay particular attention to the face, back of the hands, and tops of the feet.

WHAT TO DO

Apply cool compresses if only a part of the body is involved.

Use pain medication such as acetaminophen.

Avoid spray or cream anesthetics for wide areas of burn; they can be absorbed through the skin and cause allergic reactions.

☞ SEE YOUR PEDIATRICIAN FOR

- any burn in an infant.
- any blistering burn in an older child.
- burns over a large area.

F. Cuts

Stop bleeding by applying pressure directly to the wound with a soft, dry, clean cloth. A little bit of blood can spread messily over a wide area, so what seems like a terrible amount of bleeding may turn out to come from an itsy-bitsy wound.

Sometimes it is obvious that a cut needs stitches, but many times it is not so clear. When in doubt, especially around the face, have your pediatrician check.

☞ SEE YOUR PEDIATRICIAN FOR

- any cut on the face, no matter how small.
- cuts with jagged edges, if there is a gap or hole, or if the cut is longer than a half inch.
- short but deep cuts.

G. Head Injury

Usually, if a child falls to the floor while standing, walking, or running, serious problems do not result. The situation is more dangerous if your child has a forceful blow such as from a moving swing, falls with forward motion—from a moving bike, for example—or falls from a few feet up—from a kitchen stool, a high chair, or a retaining wall.

A large and impressive goose egg on the forehead is not necessarily a sign of a serious head injury. The skin of the head and face has a rich blood supply, and even trivial injuries can cause dramatic swelling. What is more important is how your child acts after a fall.

If your child cries and yells, wait a few minutes for everything to calm down. Remember, it is highly unlikely that a vigorously crying child is unconscious or having difficulty breathing.

A common misconception is that children should not be allowed to go to sleep after a head injury. For heaven's sake, if it is naptime or bedtime, or your child just calmed down from fifteen minutes of screaming, sleep is in order. Just check every fifteen to thirty minutes that your child has not thrown up, is breathing easily, and seems rousable.

If your child was knocked out, however briefly, even if she woke up right away, go to your pediatrician's office or an emergency room. Often children who were knocked out are kept overnight for observation. If your child loses consciousness some time later, or does not waken in a few seconds, call the emergency squad for immediate attention and careful transportation to the emergency room.

A second head injury that occurs before a child is fully recovered from the first one can be devastating, so be sure your child is completely back to normal after a head injury before returning to competitive sports. Depending on the severity of the injury, that may be days or weeks.

☎ CALL YOUR PEDIATRICIAN AFTER A HEAD INJURY FOR

- vomiting.
- fluid drainage from the nose or ear.
- unequal pupils.
- weakness of one side of the body.
- difficulty walking or talking.
- a headache that gets worse and worse.
- confusion or diminishing alertness.

☞ TAKE YOUR CHILD TO AN EMERGENCY ROOM FOR

· any loss of consciousness with the injury.

☎ CALL THE EMERGENCY SQUAD IF

· your child remains unconscious.

· your child loses consciousness some time after the injury.

H. Mouth Injuries

i. *Knocked-Out Tooth*

The tooth that children most commonly knock out is one of the top incisors right in the front. Toddlers from eighteen to thirty months lose their replaceable baby teeth when they stagger around and fall on their faces learning to walk and run. Later, children around nine to ten years who are beginning to play competitive sports can lose permanent teeth. Not surprisingly, boys are twice as likely to knock out a permanent tooth as girls.

WHAT TO DO

A baby tooth does not need to be replaced. A space in the front of the mouth may be cosmetically troublesome for a while, but a permanent tooth will fill it in a few years.

If a permanent tooth is knocked out, the faster it is replaced in its socket, the more likely it is that it will reattach itself and be healthy. If the tooth is replaced in its socket within thirty minutes, there is a 90 percent chance that it will successfully reattach. Between thirty and ninety minutes, the chances decrease to 40 percent, and if it takes longer than ninety minutes, the chances for saving the tooth are less than one in ten.

Wash the tooth gently under running water, but do not scrub it or you may remove tissue vital for reattachment.

If you cannot replace the tooth right away, try to keep it moist. Have your child spit into a cup and transport the tooth covered with saliva, or put it in a clean container covered with milk. If neither of these is possible, a child who is old enough not to swallow the tooth can keep it in the fold between the lower lip and the gums while you seek medical or dental assistance.

☞ **SEE YOUR PEDIATRICIAN IF**

· you cannot reinsert the tooth yourself within thirty minutes.

☞ **SEE YOUR DENTIST IF**

· a replaced tooth becomes discolored or painful.

ii. Shoved-In Tooth

In younger children it is more common for a baby tooth to be pushed up into the gum than to be knocked out. Most of the time, the tooth will resume its normal position in three to four weeks.

WHAT TO DO

Leave the tooth alone unless it looks severely out of place. If it does not resume its normal position in three to four weeks, it may have to be extracted because it will obstruct the normal path of the permanent tooth.

☞ **SEE YOUR PEDIATRIC DENTIST IF**

· there is tenderness with eating a week or so after the tooth was shoved in; an abcess may have developed.

iii. Bleeding Mouth

When your child falls face first and runs in with blood all over himself, chances are it is only due to a tear in the little piece of tissue that attaches the inside of the upper lip to the space between the front teeth. This *frenulum* is particularly prone to injury and can bleed briskly for a few minutes, but it is not a serious problem.

WHAT TO DO

Apply pressure with a cloth, or if your child will not let you do that, offer a Popsicle or some cold object to suck on to stop the bleeding.

☞ SEE YOUR PEDIATRICIAN IF

- bleeding will not stop after fifteen minutes.
- an injury to the mouth involved a sharp object.
- any injury might have penetrated the roof of the mouth.
- bleeding comes from the gum around the base of a tooth.

| 3 | BROKEN BONES |

A. Is It Broken?

Unless one end of the bone is obviously going north while the other is headed west, there is no fool-proof way to tell if a bone is broken. Sprains can swell more than fractures; children may continue to use a broken arm, and even x-rays may not show a small fracture right away.

Rules of thumb: Usually a fracture will be extremely tender if you press directly on the broken area. Children rarely let a minor injury stop them from playing for more than a few minutes, while a broken bone will make a child slow down and avoid pressure on the bone after the injury.

There is a complicating factor with children's bones that is not present in adults: If the growth center is damaged, there is a chance for permanent deformity or impaired function, so possible fractures should be diagnosed and treated promptly.

☞ SEE YOUR PEDIATRICIAN FOR

- any possible fracture.

☎ CALL YOUR PEDIATRICIAN *IMMEDIATELY* IF THERE IS

- a history of previous swelling in the affected area.
- fever or recent illness associated with pain.
- warmth or redness in the area of the injury.

B. Specific Bone Injuries

i. *Collarbone*

Broken collarbones come from blows to the shoulder or from falling sideways. Children too young to talk are reluctant to move the arm on the injured side; older children can tell you that their shoulder hurts, and pressing on the outer edge of the collarbone causes pain.

Except for rare cases when the ends of the bone are in severe misalignment, broken collarbones heal without

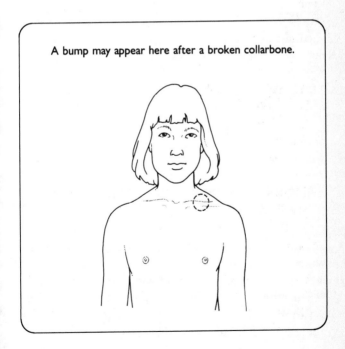

A bump may appear here after a broken collarbone.

any treatment. Your pediatrician may fit your child with a brace to keep the shoulder back, but that is more for comfort than positioning the bone.

A week or two after the injury, you may notice a hard lump protruding from your child's collarbone. That is a normal part of the healing process, but it may take several months to even out.

ii. Arm

The two most common bone injuries to children's arms are a break in the radius—the big bone of the forearm—or a pulled elbow—nursemaid's elbow or dislocated radial head.

BROKEN BONE

Since children's bones are growing and supple like the branches of a young tree, trauma to the forearm can cause a *greenstick* fracture, in which the bones are weakened but not separated, just as a green twig can be bent but not broken. This must be splinted or casted for protection from further injury, but it heals quickly. There may be minimal pain unless you press directly on the area of the fracture, which is usually near the wrist.

This type of broken bone often is diagnosed a day or two after the injury because the pain is only moderate, not severe.

NURSEMAID'S ELBOW, DISLOCATED RADIAL HEAD

Pulling on the arm of a small child in play or wrenching a recalcitrant child across the street can temporarily widen the joint space in the elbow and catch a ligament between two bones. The child will hold his arm slightly flexed with the wrist limp, and any attempt to move the arm is met with cries of pain, although the arm does not seem to hurt when it is held still.

Your pediatrician can perform a simple maneuver to return the joint to a normal position. Although I was once able to tell a dentist father over the phone how to relocate his child's arm while they were out camping, usually parents prefer to come into the office to have me do it.

There is no need for a cast or splint for the first injury, but if this keeps happening, your doctor may recommend splinting the arm for a few days or consultation with an orthopedist.

See also page 191 in Chapter VII, "Bones and Joints."

iii. Nose

A swollen, bruised nose may or may not be broken, but this is one of the few fractures that does not need to be treated immediately. If your child fell face first or got clobbered by a baseball, your pediatrician will test the stability of the nose and look for signs of bleeding into the wall that separates the two nostrils. Much of your child's nose is cartilage and not bone, so a break may not show up on an x-ray right away. If there is a fracture, you will see evidence of healing on the x-ray by five to ten days after the injury.

Unless there are complicated injuries to other facial bones, surgeons prefer to wait five days or so before they even see a child with a broken nose.

Fever

Fever is the reason for most phone calls to pediatricians and for as many as one out of five visits that children and their parents make to a pediatrician's office or an emergency facility. Parents can easily be frightened by fever, especially because the highest temperatures tend to occur at night, when everything is scarier. The vast majority of times, however, a high fever comes from nothing more than a minor viral infection.

Infants under two months are an exception. Any fever at this age is serious until proven otherwise and must be seen by your pediatrician. See Chapter I, "The Newborn," pages 19–47.

Every child is bound to have a fever sometime. It will help reduce any fear of fever you might have and increase your sense of control if you know what to expect, how to help your child to feel better, and when there might be a serious problem. Also, you should know how to react to a fever convulsion before you see one.

· WHAT IS A FEVER? ·

In a baby under three months old, any temperature over 100.5°F (38°C) is a fever. In addition, a temperature *under* 97.5°F (36.4°C) in that age group is a cause for concern. Small infants have trouble regulating their body temperature when they are sick and can just as likely drop as raise their body temperature in response to infection.

Over age three months, 101°F is the cutoff. Although 98.6°F is considered "normal," readings can be as low as 97°F in the early morning or 100.5°F in the evening. Not only does body temperature vary with the time of day, but it goes up when children have been playing hard, especially when it is a warm day. Be sure your child has been sitting quietly for fifteen to thirty minutes before you measure her temperature.

· FACTS ABOUT FEVER ·

1. Fever is part of the body's normal response to invasion by germs.

2. The only reason to try to lower a fever is for your child's comfort—every fever does not need to be treated.

3. Fevers generated in the course of an illness are not in and of themselves dangerous. What is causing the fever and how sick your child looks are more important than the height of the fever.

4. A common reason that temperature does not respond to fever-reducing medication is that your child received too small a dose, so be sure to check the dose each time you give acetaminophen. (See the dosage chart on page 234.)

· MISCONCEPTIONS ABOUT FEVER ·

1. It is not true that high fevers can be dangerous.

It is not the height of a fever that creates problems but what is causing the fever in the first place. Children may generate fevers as high as 105°F in the course of a minor viral illness, or have a temperature of only 101°F during a serious illness.

What is most important is how your child looks and acts. A child with a 101°F temperature who is abnormally quiet with a vacant stare and poor color is much sicker than a child with a 103°F fever who is running around and playing.

Fevers of 107°F or 108°F can lead to brain damage, but these temperatures are usually generated by exposure to extreme heat, such as when children are accidentally locked in a car on a hot day.

2. It is not true that a fever that does not come down with medicine is more serious than one that responds to acetaminophen.

For many years pediatricians have been trying to find consistent criteria to determine which children are more likely to have a serious cause for their fever and which ones can be safely watched for a while. It seems logical that a serious infection should not respond to simple antifever measures as readily as a minor one. Unfortunately, that is not the case. Children with serious infections are just as likely to drop their temperature with medication as are those with a minor illness.

What turns out to be important in every study of fever in children is that a combination of factors including age, duration of fever, other symptoms such as vomiting, some lab tests such as white blood count, and above all else, *how the child looks* determines the likelihood of a serious problem.

3. It is not true that a fever convulsion can cause brain damage.

When a convulsion starts, a child usually becomes stiff, the eyes roll back, and the mouth clamps shut or makes smacking noises. Twitching of all four limbs may follow. During this time your child's lips and face may turn blue. After the seizure is over, usually in less than five to ten minutes, most children sleep for a while—perhaps five to thirty minutes.

It is understandable to think that such a cataclysm must cause some damage, but fortunately it does no lasting harm.

Nobody knows exactly what causes children to go into convulsions. There are certain infections, such as roseola (see page 172), which are more often associated with them than others. Since convulsions have occurred at temperatures no higher than 101°F, some experts think that it is as often the rate at which the temperature rises as the height it reaches that can set off a convulsion.

4. It is not true that treating a fever early will prevent a fever convulsion.

This misconception can give parents jangled nerves and high anxiety and can lead to overtreating fevers. Anyone who has witnessed one fever convulsion never wants to see another, but unfortunately, there is really no way to prevent it.

Approximately one third of all healthy, normal children who have had one seizure will have another, and 10 percent will have three or more.

The older your child is at the time of the first seizure, the less likely it is that there will be more. Those who have their first seizure before age one have a 50 percent chance of having another, and the risk declines steadily thereafter. Fortunately, if there hasn't been a second seizure within two years, your child is unlikely to experience any more, and by age five you are out of the woods.

5. It is not true that treating a fever might impair the body's ability to fight infection.

Although fever is one part of the body's defenses against infection, lowering a fever does not impair children with normal immune systems. If your child is uncomfortable with a fever, you won't do any harm by trying to lower it.

· HOW TO TAKE YOUR CHILD'S TEMPERATURE ·

Electronic, mercury, or forehead strips?
Mercury and glass thermometers have been with us for centuries and are reliable tools. Unfortunately, many people find them difficult to read, and it takes several minutes to obtain an accurate reading in a wiggly, upset child.

Electronic thermometers are easy to read, have become reasonably priced, and are fast as well as accurate. The problem is that electronic thermometers rely on batteries which have a way of expiring without warning at the most inopportune times. Keep a mercury thermometer on hand just in case.

Temperature-sensitive chemical strips that you place on your child's forehead or that turn colors on a pacifier are notoriously unreliable. Your hands or lips are probably just as good or better than those gadgets.

If you use a mercury thermometer, be sure it is shaken down below 98.6°F before you start.

Armpit, mouth, or rectum?
Whichever method you use, forget whatever you have heard about correcting the reading a degree more or less when taking armpit versus rectal temperatures.

The truth is there are no consistent differences among the three ways to take a temperature. And it really doesn't matter whether your child's temperature is 102.8°F or 103.2°F. The important thing is to take it the same way each time in order to see if it is going up or down.

If you took an armpit or oral temperature and it does

not seem correct based on how hot your child feels to your touch, you can check it with a rectal temperature.

1. How to Take a Rectal Temperature

The most accurate temperature is a rectal one, but don't attempt it unless you are sure of what you are doing. It is usually best to have two people available if you are trying this in an infant or toddler who is reluctant to hold still.

Lubricate the bulb of a glass and mercury or electronic thermometer with a little petroleum jelly or K-Y jelly. While holding your child firmly facedown, insert the bulb just barely past the silver tip, slightly less than one inch.

Hold it in place for one to two minutes with one hand while holding your child still with the other.

2. How to Take an Axillary (Armpit) Temperature

Axillary, or armpit, temperatures are less accurate but safer than rectal ones if your child is especially wiggly or if you are not experienced taking a rectal temperature. Axillary temperature is inaccurate right after a bath

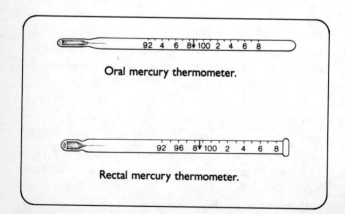

Oral mercury thermometer.

Rectal mercury thermometer.

when the skin might be temporarily cooled by evaporation.

You can use either an oral, rectal, or electronic thermometer.

Make sure the armpit is dry and there is no clothing between the skin and the thermometer.

Place the tip of the thermometer high up in the armpit, bring the arm down alongside the body and hold your child snugly for four to five minutes. Rocking or humming can help keep your child quiet for those seemingly interminable minutes.

3. How to Take an Oral Temperature

An oral temperature is feasible only if your child is over five years old. Make sure your child has not drunk any hot or cold liquids for fifteen to thirty minutes before you begin.

Place the long, slender tip of the oral thermometer under your child's tongue on either side.

Have your child close the lips without biting on the thermometer and wait for two to three minutes.

· HOW TO TREAT A FEVER ·

The cardinal rule is to do what makes your child most comfortable. If your child is hot and flushed or sweating, take off everything but underwear or diapers so that the body can lose heat through the skin more easily. On the other hand, if your child has a shaking chill, pile on the blankets until the shivering stops. Keep the room at a comfortable temperature—about the usual 72 degrees.

A bath in lukewarm water or a cool washcloth on the forehead might help, but be careful not to cool your child's skin too quickly. If you do, goosebumps and

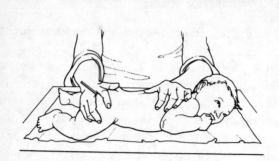

a. Position for a rectal temperature.

b. Position for an armpit (axillary) temperature.

shivering may paradoxically raise your child's temperature instead of lowering it.

Nobody feels like eating in the midst of a raging fever, but little sips of clear fluids such as juice, bits of Popsicle, or pieces of Jell-O may feel good. While it is true that children should be encouraged to take liquids when they are sick, you are more likely to get something down if you wait until the fever dips a bit and your child feels a little better. If you try to force milk or solid foods, you may increase the chances of vomiting.

Avoid rubbing your child with alcohol. The fumes can make both you and your child sick, especially if you use it in a small room. Lukewarm water works just as well without any danger.

Medications

The safest drug to use is acetaminophen, the active ingredient in Tylenol, Tempra, Liquiprin, Panadol, etc. Not only is there a wide margin of safety and low incidence of side effects, but it is the only over-the-counter antifever medication available in liquid form suitable for infants and small children.

Aspirin was the traditional fever reducer for hundreds of years, but it comes only as chewable or swallowable tablets.

A more serious drawback to aspirin is that it can cause *Reye's syndrome*, a potentially fatal brain and liver problem seen especially with flu and chicken pox.

Do not give your child aspirin except under the direct orders and supervision of your pediatrician. Remember, too, that some over-the-counter drugs may contain aspirin.

Your pediatrician may prescribe liquid ibuprofen for fever control. Although it has been used for children for only a few years, it appears to more effective in some children than acetaminophen. Whether it will prove to be as safe as acetaminophen remains to be seen.

Dosage Chart for Acetaminophen

This chart is based on children of average weight for age. If your nine-month-old is the size of a one-year-old, adjust the dose accordingly.

Doses can be given every four to six hours, and you will almost certainly have to repeat the dose. Do not expect that your child's temperature will drop to normal levels immediately. In one to two hours, you may achieve enough of a drop to make your child more comfortable—the major purpose of treatment.

If your child is sleeping comfortably, there is no need to wake her up for a middle-of-the-night dose.

| | \multicolumn{7}{c}{A G E} |
Form	0–3 mos	4–11 mos	12–13 mos	2–3 yrs	4–5 yrs	6–8 yrs	9–10 yrs
Drops (droppersful)	½	1	1½	2			
Elixir (tsp)		½	¾	1	1½	2	3
Chewable tabs			1½	2	3	4	5
Jr. strength swallowable						2	3
Adult tablets					1	1½	2

Dosage chart for Acetominophen

· WHAT TO DO FOR A FEVER CONVULSION ·

Position your child safely—preferably on the floor or bed, away from sharp corners, and out of the bathwater.

Turn your child slightly to the side so that mucus or saliva can drain out by gravity.

Do not place anything between the teeth or in the mouth; you will not prevent "swallowing the tongue" and you may do harm—break a tooth, injure your own finger, or block your child's airway.

Resist the urge to start rescue breathing (mouth-to-mouth resuscitation) until the seizure activity is stopped and your child has had a chance to resume normal breathing. Trying to do mouth-to-mouth breathing during a seizure is unneccesary and may push saliva, food, or mucus into the airway. Rescue breathing is appropriate only if your child does not start breathing a few seconds after the seizure is over.

If the twitching does not stop in ten to fifteen minutes or if your child does not resume normal breathing, call your local emergency number.

Call your pediatrician after the seizure is over for further instructions.

♥ IT IS NORMAL FOR

- children to develop a fever with minor infections.
- children to have high body temperatures when they have been running around in hot weather.
- children to have a fever for twelve to twenty-four hours after a DPT shot.
- children to be droopy or flushed when their temperature is high.
- children to hallucinate when a fever climbs.
- children's hearts to beat rapidly and forcefully when their temperature is high.
- children to breathe rapidly when their temperature is high.
- one out of twenty healthy, normal children under age five to have a fever convulsion.
- a child's temperature to be below normal sometimes, especially in the early morning or when recovering from a virus.

☎ CALL YOUR PEDIATRICIAN IF

- your infant is under three months and has a fever over 100.5°F taken twice one hour apart.
- the fever has lasted more than forty-eight hours, especially if there is no obvious cause.
- your child has had a fever convulsion.

☞ SEE YOUR PEDIATRICIAN OR GO TO AN EMERGENCY ROOM **IMMEDIATELY** IF

- your child with a fever
  - is crying inconsolably.
  - has a weak cry.
  - is abnormally quiet with a vacant stare.
  - is difficult to arouse.
  - acts as though it hurts to move or be moved.
  - is grunting, moaning, or making an "uh" sound with each breath or is having difficulty breathing.

- is breathing faster than forty breaths a minute even after fever is down.
- your child's temperature remains over 104°F for two or more hours despite your efforts to bring it down.
- fever is accompanied by vomiting.
- fever is associated with any kind of rash.
- your child has a fever convulsion which lasts longer than fifteen minutes, or she does not wake up and act normal shortly afterward.
- your child has a chronic medical condition such as diabetes or severe asthma.
- your child was recently exposed to a serious illness, such as meningitis in a day-care classmate.

Habits &

Behaviors

| 1 | HABITS AND MANNERISMS |

A. Thumbsucking

Infants must suck in order to survive—that is the way they eat. But the act of sucking serves more complicated purposes than merely nutrition. Between feedings, sucking a thumb or pacifier helps a baby who is hurt, sick, upset, or bored to feel soothed and more comfortable.

Ultrasound pictures from as early as three months before birth show that infants suck their thumbs while they are still in the uterus. By the way, it is not always a thumb. Your baby may prefer any other finger or combination of fingers. One of my patients sucked on her left forearm—so much so that she had a persistent "hickey" there until she stopped.

Almost 50 percent of all three- to four-year-olds suck their thumbs. The number drops to about one out of fifteen by age six. Since most older children are embarrassed to do it in front of their playmates, they will often suck only when they are alone, when falling asleep, or riding in the car. Thumbsucking can continue secretly even long after that. One of my adult friends confessed to me that he sucked his thumb well into his teens. The only problem was that, as an active boy, his one thumb was always suspiciously clean compared to the rest of his hands.

Some people think that thumbsucking leads to nail biting later, but that is not true. It does seem, however, that children who have sucked their thumbs are more likely at a later age to chew pencils or rub their lips when they are concentrating.

The advantage of thumbsucking over a pacifier as far as parents are concerned is that children can always find their thumbs. Nobody has to get up in the middle of the night to find it for them. On the other hand, when it is time to stop, you can throw away a pacifier but not a thumb.

Parents and dentists become concerned about the damage that thumbsucking may do to the configuration of a child's teeth. Although baby teeth might be pushed forward, if your child stops sucking by the time permanent teeth erupt or restricts it only to bedtime or perhaps a few quiet moments while at home, chances are good that there will not be any permanent dental deformity.

If your child is over five and needs to suck for comfort and relief of tension, by all means let it continue. It is futile to try to get children to stop sucking unless they are motivated to do so themselves. Remember that it is much easier to repair a dental malocclusion than to repair a damaged psyche.

Sometimes, however, thumbsucking continues not because it fills a need but just because it is a habit. A seven-year-old patient of mine was the pitcher for his Little League team. He was such a habit sucker that he would take his hand out of his mitt between pitches so he could suck his thumb. In that case, discuss trying to stop with your child. Your pediatrician will have some concrete suggestions to help, but be sure you use only positive methods—rewarding abstinence rather than punishing sucking.

♥ IT IS NORMAL FOR

• children to suck their thumbs regularly up to age four and even at later ages at bedtime and times of stress.

☎ CALL YOUR PEDIATRICIAN IF

• your child is still sucking regularly and habitually when permanent teeth erupt to determine positive strategies that can help discourage the behavior.

B. Nail Biting

Nail biting can start as early as age five to six and, unlike most other childhood habits, can persist throughout life. Children who sucked their thumbs are no more likely to become nail biters than those who haven't.

Although this habit, like all others, serves to release tension, it is not necessarily a sign that your child is abnormally stressed. Nail biting creates an increased chance for infections around the nails and your child's hands may not be as attractive as you would like, but more serious problems do not result from it.

The chances of controlling this habit are better if your child cooperates enthusiastically. A reward or incentive system such as the promise of a professional manicure for your daughter if her nails grow out or a small amount of money for each day or week without nail biting can help. If your child really wants to stop, ask your pediatrician about using the bitter liquid (such as Thum or Stop-zit) that is used for reminding children when they are thumbsucking, but only if your child wants the reminder.

♥ IT IS NORMAL FOR

• children to start biting their nails anytime during childhood and to continue for many years.

☎ CALL YOUR PEDIATRICIAN IF

- there is a problem with recurrent infections of the nail bed.
- your child wants help in stopping.

C. Hair Twirling and Pulling

Some childhood habits turn out to have been a part of a parent's childhood also. The most dramatic such history I can recall is the brother of a colleague of mine. He twirled the hair on his right temple with his thumb and second and third fingers through his early childhood. His daughter, who is now 6, started doing exactly the same thing at 10 months, and his son, now 2½, started doing it at 18 months!

Hair twirling is a little like thumbsucking—children tend to do it mostly when they are bored or going to sleep. They may twirl with one hand and suck a thumb or hold a blanket with the other. Persistent twirling can lead to a patch of thinning hair or actual hair loss, but the hair usually grows back when the habit slows down.

Hair *pulling,* on the other hand, is of more concern as it may be a form of compulsive behavior. Although the scalp is the most common site, some children pull out their eyelashes and eyebrows as well.

Hair pulling may cause significant cosmetic problems with bald spots, naked eyelids, and distorted eyebrows. Hair pulling may be a sign of *obsessive-compulsive disorder* (see pages 243–44), or some other emotional disturbance which can respond to specialized treatment. If hair pulling continues longer than six months or stops but is replaced by some other repetitive behavior, ask your pediatrician for a referral to a pediatric psychiatrist or psychologist.

♥ IT IS NORMAL FOR

- children to twirl hair in one place, even to the point of creating a bald spot.

⊗ IT MAY **NOT** BE NORMAL FOR

- children to pull out hair and eyelashes.

☎ CALL YOUR PEDIATRICIAN IF

- there is a rash, scaling, or itching in an area of baldness or thinning hair; it may be due to a fungus infection.
- hair pulling lasts more than six months.
- hair pulling stops but is replaced by another habit or ritual.

D. Head Banging

Starting between six and eighteen months, some children bang their heads noisily against the floor, the wall, or their crib mattress just before going to sleep or when tired or angry. They may even have a blissful expression on their face while they are doing this. Between 5 and 15 percent of all children do this at one time or another.

It is understandable that you might worry that such vigorous head banging may cause some serious injury, but the truth is this is neither harmful nor crazy. Even if there is an occasional bruise in the middle of the forehead, there is never any injury to the brain.

Presumably this behavior helps to release tension or frustration. Whatever the reason, babies who bang their heads are not psychologically disturbed or emotionally deprived unless they do it extremely frequently, if it interferes with their relationships with others, or if it replaces playtime. In these cases there may be an underlying problem.

Head banging should end by age four. There is nothing you can do to stop it, but you might put bumper pads in the crib, padding against the wall next to the crib, or extra carpet under the crib wheels to cut down on the noise it causes.

♥ IT IS NORMAL FOR

· children to bang their heads repeatedly and some-times noisily to comfort themselves or soothe them-selves to sleep.

☎ CALL YOUR PEDIATRICIAN IF

· your child starts banging the side of the head; this may indicate an ear problem.
· the habit goes on past age four.
· you think your child is spending an excessive amount of time head banging.
· your child is also doing other sorts of self-hurting behaviors.

E. Winks, Blinks, and Twitches

Sudden, repetitive, involuntary movements such as eye blinking, throat clearing, lip licking, sniffing, shrugging, sighing, and other maddening habits can plague children between four and twelve. These habits disappear during sleep and usually last less than six months.

Called simple tics or habit tics, they are most common in children from early school years until just before puberty and there is often a history of similar tics in the family. They may become more frequent during times of stress, but children can control them for short periods of time when asked to. These simple tics are not a sign of serious psychological disturbance nor are they a medical problem.

On the other hand, complex tics that involve com-binations of behavior—both grunting and blinking at the same time, finger snapping or mimicking the be-havior or words of other people, for example, or habits that last a year or more may be a sign of *Tourette's syn-drome*. In 10 percent of the children with Tourette's syn-drome, uncontrollable outbursts of obscene words or gestures are part of their tics.

In contrast to simple tics, those of Tourette's syndrome may not cease when the child falls asleep. Also, children with simple tics can control them for short periods of time. The tics of Tourette's syndrome grow worse under pressure, so asking a child to stop can sometimes cause the behavior to increase.

This neurological disorder requires consultation with a neurologist, preferably a pediatric neurologist, and can often be controlled or improved with medication.

♥ IT IS NORMAL FOR

· children between four and twelve to have simple tics lasting up to six months.

☎ CALL YOUR PEDIATRICIAN IF

· the tic is a complex behavior, is a combination of behaviors, or includes vocalizations.

· tics last more than six months, wax and wane over a long time, or a new one appears as an old one dies out.

· tics persist when your child sleeps.

· the behavior is disturbing your child because of teasing by other children.

F. Rituals: Repetitive Hand Washing, Compulsive Checking, Frequent Urination, etc.

Some compulsive rituals—"step on a crack, break your mother's back," for example—are normal and occur in a large number of children.

On the other hand, the compulsion to check and recheck the light switches, a need to count everything, or running to the sink every few minutes to wash hands or other rituals that are cumbersome and disruptive may be a sign that your child has *obsessive-compulsive disorder* (OCD). One of my patients with this disorder would do everything twice—close car doors twice, go up and down the stairs twice. He also refused to wear underwear because he said it was too tight, no matter how loose his mother made it.

Obsessive-compulsive disorder can be a mild or a crippling problem that has long been recognized in adults. We now know that it occurs in children more commonly than previously thought. Children with OCD may have an irrational fear of contamination, be obsessed with keeping their possessions in a certain order, count things repeatedly, or check hundreds of times to see if the water or light is turned off.

Many of these rituals are conducted secretly, since children know that this is not normal. The only sign of compulsive handwashing, for instance, may be raw, red hands that do not get better with hand creams, or frequent trips to the bathroom without symptoms of urinary problems. Compulsive toothbrushing may be revealed by raw sores on the gums. The only evidence of an uncontrollable impulse to check and recheck may be that your child, who always finished homework in plenty of time, now has difficulty finishing.

Under age seven, the majority of children with OCD are boys, and later in childhood the ratio changes to become about equal in girls and boys.

Fortunately, there is treatment available. Combinations of behavioral and psychological therapy and medication under the direction of a child psychiatrist can help control symptoms.

⊗ IT IS **NOT** NORMAL FOR
- children to display ritualized, repetitive behaviors.

☎ CALL YOUR PEDIATRICIAN IF
- you notice that your child is behaving rigidly and compulsively.
- you see unexplained symptoms such as raw, red hands; difficulty finishing homework or leaving the house; etc.

- your child expresses one or a series of irrational fears that persist and interfere with daily life.

| 2 | SLEEP PROBLEMS |

A child who previously slept well may begin to have difficulty getting to sleep or staying in bed at times of stress or change: when your family is going through a move or a divorce, when Mother returns to work, when the child is having trouble at school or day-care or is going through a particularly difficult developmental spurt. (Children often have sleep problems when they begin to walk, for instance.) Once these situations are resolved, the sleep problem usually stops.

Sometimes the root of the problem simply may be bedtime routines that are stimulating rather than soothing—horseplay with Dad and the children rolling on the floor is not conducive to settling down.

On the other hand, some children have never slept through the night or they go through long periods of difficulty going to sleep or staying asleep. If your child wakens you regularly during the night but it does not bother you, there is no real problem. Many people feel that it is part of a parent's role to care for their child during the night as well as during the day and they manage to cope with that. On the other hand, if you find that *you* are chronically sleep deprived, that you are not performing well at work, and that your relationship with your spouse is on edge from lack of sleep, then you do have a problem.

This following section includes suggestions for some of the simplest and most easily solved problems. I often recommend Dr. Richard Ferber's practical and helpful book, *Solving Your Child's Sleep Problems*. If the simple measures here or in his book do not help, see your pediatrician for a more detailed and personal approach. A large proportion of bedtime struggles are tangled webs of individual needs and responses of parents and their children, and require some special attention.

A. Going to Bed

Children between ages four and six may be afraid to go to bed because of monsters hiding in the closet or bears or witches that will "get them" once the light goes out. A night light is not the answer; in fact, sometimes it makes things worse because of the shadows it casts.

Though the monsters are not real, the fears are, and just poo-poohing them is not likely to reassure your child. My head nurse, Jeannie, had a loving and creative solution when her daughter wouldn't go to sleep because of "ghosts." Besides reassuring Stacy that no harm would come to her, Jeannie bought a special can of ghost spray (air freshener), and sprayed the windows and doors of Stacy's room each night before turning off the light. She also left a can at Stacy's bedside and told her she could use it if she woke up afraid.

The problem cleared up in a short time, as it might have anyway, but Stacy was given a way to overcome her fear and, more important, a message that her feelings counted.

♥ IT IS NORMAL FOR

· children ages four to six to have some fears about going to bed.

☎ CALL YOUR PEDIATRICIAN IF

· these fears do not go away in a few weeks.
· the fears are so great that they persist during the day as well.

B. Getting Out of Bed, Sleeping with Parents

Children who get out of bed and climb in with their parents usually are lonesome, frightened, or in need of some reassurance. This behavior often begins around the time a second child is born, for example. Although some child-care experts consider it a capital crime, personally, I see nothing wrong with letting your child get into bed with you once in a while—at times of special need or illness. An early-morning family cuddle is also wonderful.

Problems arise, however, when children ask to join you every night. If you are a single parent, be sure you do not start using your child to provide company in your lonely bed. Not only is this psychologically unhealthy, but difficult problems can arise when you do take another adult into your bed and throw the child out.

It is also hard for a parent to perform at work after a sleepless night being kicked and punched by a thrashing child.

One possible solution is to make a place for your child on the floor next to your bed to curl up on during the night while, during that same period, you reward those nights your child spends in bed alone. Sleeping on the floor does no harm—the Japanese do it all their lives. My friend Charley is now twenty-one years old, and spent many nights of his early childhood curled up on a red throw rug. He is a normal, healthy, and happy adult now.

Another possible solution is to take your child back to his own bed but sit next to it with your hand gently on your child's back until drowsiness takes over.

♥ IT IS NORMAL FOR
 • children to want to get into bed with their parents.
 • parents to take their children into bed on special occasions or for an early-morning cuddle.

⊗ IT IS **NOT** HEALTHY FOR
 • children to sleep with their parents all the time.

C. Night Waking

Although some parents are lucky enough to have a baby that sleeps through the night from birth, most infants wake up one to three times during the night for most of the first year. Twenty to thirty percent of all children between ages one and five wake up at least once during the night, also.

Parents often ask if feeding their infant cereal at bedtime would help their child to sleep longer. Unfortunately, it does not. Infants sleep through the night when they are developmentally ready to and not before.

The most common reason infants and toddlers waken more often than normal during the night is that they never learned how to get themselves to sleep. Children who are rocked or fed at bedtime and put into their cribs fully asleep will need that same feeling to get back to sleep when they go through normal waking cycles later at night.

The problem is easier to prevent than to solve. Be sure that your child is drowsy but still awake when you leave him in his crib and go out the door. If you already have this problem now, you might solve it by gradually decreasing the time you spend putting your child to sleep and laying your child down a little more awake each night.

♥ IT IS NORMAL FOR

- infants to wake up several times a night during the first year.

☎ CALL YOUR PEDIATRICIAN IF

- you cannot get your child to bed without being fully asleep.

D. Sleepwalking and Sleep Talking

Fifteen percent of all children between ages five and twelve have sleepwalked at least once, and 10 percent of them do it regularly. A child who sleepwalks climbs out of bed and makes a clumsy, purposeless walk through the house. There may be some confused behavior, such as walking into a closet as though it were the bathroom. What happened during the night is not remembered the next morning.

There is no need to do anything about sleepwalking except to make sure your child is safe from injury and cannot leave the house. Merely lead your child back to bed gently.

Talking during sleep is even more common than sleepwalking. Usually monosyllabic nonsense words come out in a mumbling voice, although sometimes a child will grow vociferous and articulate. This usually happens during dreams. Although this may disrupt *your* sleep, there is no need to waken your child or do anything else about it.

♥ IT IS NORMAL FOR
- children to sleepwalk and sleep talk.

☎ CALL YOUR PEDIATRICIAN IF
- you have trouble making sure your child is safe.
- there are any other sleep problems.

E. Nightmares and Night Terrors

Nightmares are bad dreams from which children awaken frightened. They can usually recall their dream at the time as well as in the morning. Generally nightmares need only reassurance and a hug and your child will go back to sleep. Most children will have a nightmare once in a while, and they may become more frequent at times of stress. They serve an important psychological function, and as long as they are not frequent or regular or cause your child to be afraid to go to sleep, just provide reassurance.

Just as normal as nightmares but more frightening to parents who are unfamiliar with them are "night terrors," which occur in children between about ages two and six. The child seems to be awake because both eyes are wide open and words are coming out, but the child is agitated, unaware of your presence, and makes no sense. Despite appearances, the child is actually still asleep.

The four-year-old son of a pediatrician I know was banging on the wall next to his bed and yelling strange things one night. My friend said, "Jonathon, it's me, I'm your mother." He looked at her with wide open eyes and said, "I know you. You're a big, hairy gorilla."

Night terrors can last up to a half hour. During that time, you will have little luck trying to either calm or waken your child, who will not remember anything about what happened by the morning.

Night terrors are not a sign that your child is abnormally fearful. They are thought to be due to a peculiar state of arousal that children pass through during the night at this age, and they will stop on their own.

♥ IT IS NORMAL FOR

· children to have occasional nightmares at any age and night terrors between two and six.

☎ CALL YOUR PEDIATRICIAN FOR

· persistent nightmares that do not go away.
· fear of nightmares that is preventing your child from going to sleep.
· night terrors that start over the age of five or multiple attacks that are persistent.

| 3 | EATING |

A. Not Eating or Eating Only One or Two Foods

Once past infancy, toddlers sometimes go through periods when they seem to be living on nothing but air and water. Your active, growing child refuses whatever food you offer, yet still has enough energy to run you ragged. Later on, that same child may go through food fads—eating only mayonnaise and bologna on white bread, or frozen corn kernels and hot dogs for a week or more at a time.

Do not panic. Malnutrition will not set in. Although we all learned that we should eat from the four basic food groups every day, nutritional and caloric needs vary from person to person, from age to age, and from day to day. When children go through their next growth spurt, they are likely to start eating better.

Active children may eat several small snacks through the day more readily than three large meals. Being a toddler is a little like being in an all-day marathon. Constant, intense physical activity does not make you crave a heavy meal like steak and a baked potato but, rather, frequent, small snacks for ongoing energy.

It helps if you familiarize yourself with nutritional substitutions. A child who refuses any green vegetable can receive similar nutrition from cantaloupe, apricots, corn, or sweet potatoes, for example. Children who refuse milk will almost always accept pudding, yogurt, or chocolate milk.

Vitamins do not make up for missing food. It is virtually impossible for healthy American children to become vitamin deficient no matter how crazily they eat for a few weeks. Nevertheless, if it makes *you* feel better to give vitamins, you won't do any harm if you use a preparation formulated for children and give only the recommended dose.

♥ IT IS NORMAL FOR

- toddlers to go through periods of refusing most food.
- preschool children to eat only selected foods for weeks at a time.

☎ **CALL YOUR PEDIATRICIAN IF**

• your child seems to be losing weight, is not as active as usual while refusing food, or has any other signs of being ill.

B. Appetite for Abnormal Substances: Paint, Dirt, etc.

One of my favorite phone messages was, "Mrs. Stone is on the phone. Jeremy is eating her couch." It turned out he had found a hole in the upholstery and was eating the stuffing.

Children will put almost anything in their mouths because they use their mouths as well as their hands and eyes to explore the world. When they habitually eat nonnutritive materials, however, it may be a sign of an underlying problem, most commonly an iron deficiency.

In addition, eating old, flaking paint chips or dirt risks lead poisoning, which causes neurological and developmental problems. This behavior, called *pica,* is seen most commonly in children between two and five.

⊗ IT IS *NOT* NORMAL FOR

• children to have a constant appetite for strange substances.

☎ **CALL YOUR PEDIATRICIAN IF**

• your child repeatedly eats what shouldn't be eaten.

| 4 | BLADDER AND BOWEL CONTROL |

A. Refusal to Toilet Train for Urine

Most children are ready to be toilet trained between eighteen months and three years. A popular misconception is that all two-year-olds are toilet trained, and that is far from true. Girls are in general a little faster than boys, but there is a lot of individual variation. Children who take a little longer to learn to use the toilet are not any more or less intelligent than ones who are trained at eighteen months. Allow your children to follow their own timetable.

Your child needs to be physically, developmentally, and intellectually ready for toilet training. Physical readiness means that your child can be dry for several hours at a time, empties the bladder completely when urinating, and can tell you when the urge to urinate begins. Developmentally, a child should be able to do some complex maneuvers such as pulling pants up and down, walk well, and handle small objects with some dexterity. Intellectually, a child must be able to understand and follow instructions.

When your child seems ready in all these ways, it is still a good idea to wait three months more. The rapidity of toilet training is not as important psychologically as how smoothly it is done, so waiting ensures that it will be easier for everyone.

A child who is physically able to control these functions may not be ready emotionally, and pushing only makes things worse. Not infrequently, for example, when a second child is born and the first child is between two and three years, there is little incentive for child number one to achieve the independence that accompanies knowing how to use the toilet while Mommy and Daddy are focusing their attention on the new baby. You get a lot more attention having your diapers changed than going to the potty by yourself.

Even children who are perfectly dry all day may continue to wet at night until age six or later. See the section on bedwetting, page 129.

♥ IT IS NORMAL FOR
- some children to need longer for successful toilet training.
- children to wet during the night long after successful daytime toilet training.

- your child is over 3½ and still cannot be trained.
- your child was trained but now is having accidents.

B. Accidents with Stool, Soiling

About three out of a hundred young children have difficulty controlling stool or having a bowel movement in the toilet. A three-year-old who is perfectly able to urinate in the toilet may refuse to have a bowel movement anywhere but in a diaper. Even when in training pants, he will ask for a diaper and then go into another room to pass the stool.

Sometimes this behavior is caused by fear. It may be fear of the pain that accompanied a hard, constipated stool, fear of the monster that lives in the toilet and can noisily gobble up children when it is flushed, or fear of falling in because your child's feet cannot rest comfortably when sitting on an adult toilet seat.

A child who was previously able to have a bowel movement in the toilet and then had a hard, constipated, painful stool may withhold stool for fear it will hurt. As more and more stool accumulates in the rectum, the child experiences overflow incontinence: loose, liquid stool seeps around the hard, accumulated material and it is difficult if not impossible to contain it.

Characteristically, when a child is withholding and having overflow problems, the stool that does finally pass is huge.

For this problem, the solution is easy. The hard, impacted stool must be cleaned out—your pediatrician can advise you about suppositories, gentle enemas, and/ or mineral oil. After that, increased fiber, decreased dairy products, stool softeners, and other measures to make sure stool remains easy to pass prevents a recurrence of the situation. (See the section on constipation, pages 102–4.)

About fifty percent of the time, stool accidents in a

toilet-trained child can be correlated with a significant life event such as starting school, the birth of a new baby, or separating from Mommy. In each case, the accidents usually stop once the emotional upset has subsided.

If your child has always been constipated, is gaining weight poorly, has abdominal pain, and passes small-diameter stools, be sure to bring that to your doctor's attention. These could be signs of *Hirschsprung's disease,* a disorder in which the nerves to the rectum are deficient.

⊗ IT IS **NOT** NORMAL FOR

- a child who was previously able to control stool to be incontinent, although it may be due to an easily solved problem.

☞ SEE YOUR PEDIATRICIAN FOR

- a complete history and physical if your child is repeatedly unable to control stool.
- if there is difficulty passing stool that dates from infancy and that is associated with abdominal pain, small-size stools, and/or poor weight gain.

☞ SEE YOUR PEDIATRICIAN **IMMEDIATELY** IF

- stool accidents are associated with fever, abdominal pain, bloody stool, or any other signs of illness.

| 5 | DEVELOPMENTAL PROBLEMS |

A. Slow Motor Development, Delayed Walking

Although the average age at which a child begins to walk is twelve months, some children walk by nine months and some wait until fifteen to sixteen months. It has *nothing* to do with intelligence.

Often children who start to walk late come from a

family in which other people walked late. Before you worry, ask aunts, uncles, and grandparents if there is a history of late walking in the family.

If your child is "cruising," that is, pulling up independently and walking around holding on to furniture, there is less cause for concern than if your child is just sitting without making an effort to rise. Hip problems can make walking painful or clumsy, or mild neurological problems may go unnoticed until a child refuses to walk.

♥ IT IS NORMAL FOR

· walking to be delayed until fifteen or sixteen months in some children.

☞ SEE YOUR PEDIATRICIAN IF

· your child is not walking by fifteen months.

· your child is up and cruising but walking seems difficult—unsteadiness, limping, keeping one leg bent, etc.

· you notice any other subtle signs that development is not proceeding normally.

B. Clumsiness

Before you label your child as clumsy, be sure your expectations are not out of line. Coordination can have a different timetable in each child, and some tasks may be mastered early while others are late. Some broad parameters are:

	Average	When to worry
Walking	12 months	15 months
Walk upstairs	18 months	22 months
Balance on one foot		
1 second	2½ years	3½ years
10 seconds	5 years	6 years
Copy a circle	2½ years	3½ years
Copy a square	5 years	7 years

It is more significant if a child does several tasks poorly than if there is only one giving trouble. Eric, a patient who is now in his twenties and has always been a gifted student, was singled out by his first-grade teacher because he could not skip. He did everything else well, however. She raised unnecessary worries in his parents because of one developmental task that he failed. He still is not able to skip, although he graduated from law school with honors.

The most common cause of chronic clumsiness is the "clumsy child syndrome," or in more medical-sounding terms, congenital maladroitness. These children have trouble running, fall frequently, are poor athletes, have terrible handwriting, and may even have trouble dressing themselves. It is important to diagnose this for two reasons. First, teachers and coaches should not expect more from these children than they are able to do, and second, there are often associated learning disabilities which should be diagnosed and treated as early as possible. If clumsiness increases, there may be an underlying neurologic problem.

If your child has been developing normally but suddenly starts to be clumsy, see your pediatrician right away. There may be a serious problem, although mild viral infections in a part of the brain or some medications such as antihistamines can cause this as well. Some children with migraine headaches may have a period of clumsiness preceding the onset of the pain.

♥ IT IS NORMAL FOR
   · children to be clumsy when learning a new skill.

☞ SEE YOUR PEDIATRICIAN IF
   · your child develops clumsiness in skills already mastered.
   · your child has always been clumsier than other children the same age.

C. Speech Problems

It is important to recognize and treat disorders of language and speech as early as possible to avoid later educational problems. Fortunately, most speech problems are correctable in under two years.

Although preschools and pediatricians can uncover problems, a study done in 1991 at Vanderbilt University confirmed that the most reliable detectors of possible problems are parents. Almost three quarters of the children who were found to have problems had parents who were already worried about their speech, and 83 percent of those with normal speech had parents who knew they were normal.

IF YOU THINK THERE IS SOMETHING WRONG WITH YOUR CHILD'S SPEECH, SEE YOUR PEDIATRICIAN EARLY. The benefits of early diagnosis far outweigh the cost of a visit.

i. Not Speaking, Delayed Speech, Unclear Speech

Before you worry that your child is late in talking, be sure your expectations are appropriate. There is a lot of variation in normal development. Here are some guidelines:

Babbling one syllable ("ba-ba-ba" or "na-na-na")	by 9 months
Several syllables	by 11 months
Mama or *Dada* used correctly	by 14 months
Single words	by 16–18 months
2-word sentences	by 2½ years
50 percent intelligible	by 22 months
Completely understandable	by 47 months

Delayed speech like delayed walking can sometimes run in families. If you did not talk until late, it is more likely that your children will speak late.

Speech may be delayed because of a hearing loss; you can't learn to speak if you can't hear the sounds. Unfortunately, hearing loss in children often goes undiagnosed for a long time. Because children learn to respond to visual and vibratory cues around them, a profound hearing loss may be present for two years before anyone notices, and children with a partial hearing loss may be four or five before it is discovered.

Even a hearing loss in only one ear can affect speech. Partial hearing loss is more likely to cause an impairment in intelligibility—making wrong sounds for letters or leaving sounds out—rather than not speaking at all.

A hearing test is painless, and no child is too young. Even newborns can be tested. Children at higher-than-average risk for hearing problems are:

- babies who were premature, who were sick as newborns, or who had an infection while in the uterus.
- children who have had meningitis.
- children born with any abnormalities of the ears, mouth, head, or neck (skin tags or small pits around the ear, etc.).
- children who have relatives who are deaf or hearing-impaired.
- children with any developmental problems.
- children who have had repeated ear infections.

If hearing is normal, and your child still has a significant delay in speech, neurological and developmental evaluations should be done.

☎ CALL YOUR PEDIATRICIAN IF

- your six-month-old does not respond to sound or has only an inconsistent response.
- your one-year-old stops babbling or has not babbled yet.
- your toddler does not use words, or your two-year-old does not make two-word phrases.
- your 2½-year-old's speech is not for the most part intelligible to the family.

- your 3-year-old is not making sentences or your 3½-year-old is not intelligible to strangers.

ii. Stuttering

A mild form of stuttering occurs in the normal course of development in 90 percent of all children between two and four years. Trouble with phrases or whole words—"I—I—I—I want to go out"—repetitions such as "I went—I went—I went to the beach," or hesitations or pauses in speech are probably due to the brain working faster than the tongue. Children with this normal form of difficulty in fluency do not appear to be struggling when they stutter. In fact, it always surprises me that they do not become more frustrated as they try to communicate. The problem usually ceases within six months.

Stuttering that is problematic generally involves sounds rather than words ("Wu—wu—wu—what is that?"). The child appears to be struggling, making faces, and obviously tensing up when trying to speak. Children with significant stuttering may actually avoid speech when possible.

Both problems may begin at the same age but normal, developmental stuttering goes away within about six months. Between 1 and 4 percent of adults have problems with stuttering, but the chances are increased three to five times if one parent stutters.

♥ IT IS NORMAL FOR

- children between ages two and four to have problems with words or parts of words for about six months.

☎ CALL YOUR PEDIATRICIAN IF

- stuttering lasts longer than six months.
- problems are with sounds rather than words or syllables.
- there is a family history of speech problems.
- your child seems to be struggling with the sounds.

6	DISCIPLINE AND BEHAVIOR PROBLEMS

A. Tantrums

I have a vivid memory of the smallest details of the black and white linoleum on the floor of the apartment my parents and I lived in until I was eight years old. The reason I do is that my face was next to it so often as I pounded my fists, screamed, and kicked in my frequent tantrums.

Many normal children between ages two and four throw themselves on the ground, kick the floor or walls, and sometimes hold their breath in a cataclysmic expression of rage and frustration. It has always seemed to me that adults would be a lot healthier if we could release tension and stress that way, but we are not allowed to. Children are.

When their desires outstrip their physical abilities, when they are denied something by their parents, or when they are unable to articulate what is bothering them, some children will explode into a tantrum. It is understandable for you to be distressed when these sessions occur in public places like the cereal aisle of the supermarket, since it seems that children instinctively know the worst possible times for us to cope with them.

Tantrums are normal, and if you can manage to be matter-of-fact about them, they will gradually decrease in frequency and disappear. If you become upset, try to stop one once it has begun, find yourself resorting to bribes to prevent a tantrum or punish your child for having one, you run the risk of prolonging their existence. If you know what is likely to set off a tantrum, you might try to head one off with diversionary tactics—present a different toy or remove the child from the situation. Once a tantrum has begun, however, children usually have to finish it before they can calm down.

♥ IT IS NORMAL FOR
· preschool-aged children to have tantrums.

☎ CALL YOUR PEDIATRICIAN IF
· tantrums do not stop by age five.
· tantrums are frequent and your child appears un-happy or disturbed much of the time.
· you are having trouble coping with your child's tantrums.

B. Passing Out After a Mild Injury or Upset; Breath-Holding Spells

Anytime between 6 months and 4 years, but most commonly between 1½ and 3, a mild injury such as a trivial blow to the head or sudden anger or frustration may precipitate a sequence of events that is actually harmless to your child but can be frightening for you.

Your child may cry out with a long, sustained wail or make no sound at all, turn blue or pale, pass out, and perhaps even twitch for a few seconds. The period of unconsciousness with or without twitching lasts ten to sixty seconds, after which your child may be slightly sleepy or quieter than usual for five to ten minutes.

The name "breath-holding spells" implies that this might be deliberate, but it is an involuntary reaction.

Although stiffness and twitching resemble a con-vulsion, these spells are not related to any neurological or brain problem. Convulsions start suddenly without any obvious cause, they last longer than a few seconds, and children usually take longer than ten minutes to recover afterward. Convulsions can occur when a child is asleep, falling asleep, or just waking up. Breath-hold-ing spells, on the other hand, are set off by an injury or a temper fit, happen only when a child is awake and aware, and last less than one minute. Furthermore, the child recovers almost immediately.

♥ IT IS NORMAL FOR

· children between six months and four years to have breath-holding spells in which they turn blue or pale, faint, and sometimes twitch.

☎ CALL YOUR PEDIATRICIAN IF

· your child is under six months or over four years when this occurs.

· the spell began without any obvious cause such as a bump, fall, or temper fit.

· the twitching or unconsciousness lasts more than sixty seconds.

· it takes your child longer than ten minutes to recover fully.

· attacks occur when your child is drowsy or asleep rather than fully awake.

C. Biting and Hitting

Biting usually starts as an exploratory behavior—children use their mouths as a sense organ just as they use their eyes and hands. They also want to try their new teeth out on animate as well as inanimate objects. By age two or three, however, what began as a game may become an aggressive expression of anger and frustration. When the few words they know fail them, biting or hitting a playmate can make their point.

When toddlers go through an emotionally trying time—when Mom goes back to work or parents are having economic or financial difficulties, for example—biting people may be their way of releasing their pent-up frustration.

Sometimes, biting may even come from an affectionate impulse without any intention of causing pain.

I shudder when I hear parents tell me that well-meaning friends or relatives counseled them to bite their child back. Not only does it make no sense for parents to display the very behavior that they are telling their child is unacceptable, but if you bite a child hard enough to hurt, you are being unnecessarily cruel.

If your breastfeeding baby bites your nipple, pull away with a sharp exclamation and then resume feeding. If your child bites a playmate, removal from the play area for a short time and a no-nonsense reprimand immediately after the episode usually works—eventually if not the first time.

Also, remember that positive messages work better than negative ones. Praise your child when playing nicely with others, and point out how proud you are when there is no biting going on.

On the other hand, you should be concerned about a child who repeatedly bites himself. Children who punish themselves are having serious problems coping with something, and should have some professional help.

The same lessons apply to hitting, kicking, and pushing other children. All children will do this at times, but if it recurs repeatedly, especially if a child seems immune to discipline, hurts other children badly, or is disliked and feared by playmates, there may be an underlying emotional problem which needs professional psychological help.

♥ IT IS NORMAL FOR

· small children to bite as a way of exploring the world or expressing frustration, and to hit, kick, or push other children once in a while.

☎ CALL YOUR PEDIATRICIAN IF

· your child is biting himself intentionally.

· agressive behavior persists for more than a few weeks after you try to stop it.

· biting has punctured a child's skin (antibiotics may be necessary depending on the location and extent of the bite, and a tetanus shot may be due).

· your child is feared or disliked by playmates because of aggressive behavior.

· your child has hurt another child badly.

D. Overactive, Not Listening, Trouble Paying Attention

Toddlers can be extremely active, running and jumping, fidgeting, speaking too quickly to be understood. When you collapse at night exhausted by your active child, you may think fondly of your sister's docile three-year-old who sits and plays quietly for hours and worry that your child is "hyperactive."

A study done at the Brookline Massachusetts Early Education Project found that 40 percent of all preschoolers were thought to have problems with high activity levels and poor ability to pay attention, but only one out of twenty turned out to have problems later in school.

A short attention span and high activity level may be normal for your child's age and level of development, but check to be sure there are no contributing factors. One of my patients, for example, drove her mother crazy with her constant activity and uncontrollable behavior. When she threw her mother's car keys down the sink in our office, we did a hearing test and found that this four-year-old could barely hear. How could she hope to mind her mother when she could not hear her instructions?

Sometimes children are distracted and overactive because of emotional upsets, especially when parents are having marital or economic problems, or the family is moving.

Some children have an inordinate amount of difficulty listening, maintaining their attention, or controlling their behavior beyond what is normal for their age. Such children may have *attention deficit disorder* (ADD).

Difficulty paying attention is most crippling to a child during the school years, when children need to pay attention, stay in their seats, and organize their work. The diagnosis of ADD can be made by your school and pediatrician working together. Treatment is complex. A lot of publicity has surrounded the use of medication, but that is only one aspect of treatment.

In a class of twenty-five children, there will be at least one child with ADD, and that child is six times more likely to be a boy than a girl. Most of the time, there are more issues beyond poor attention—perceptual problems, emotional difficulties, subtle neurological problems, or social adjustment issues are also a part of the picture. Learning disabilities, for example, may impair the child's ability to pay attention because the information the teacher presents is perceived as confusing and undecipherable.

ADD has nothing to do with intelligence. Children may be extremely bright or have serious intellectual deficits, or be anywhere in between. In fact, the brighter children are, the better able they are to work around their deficits. A bright child with ADD may go undiagnosed for years because of doing acceptable, average work even though his potential is far beyond that.

Children with ADD may have trouble getting ready for school on time, following directions—especially if they are complex—finishing schoolwork on time, controlling impulses, or keeping quiet. Because there are good days and bad days, it is common for adults to think that a child with ADD could "do it if he wanted to." The truth is, he can't.

It is important to diagnose and treat these problems as early as possible. The more positive the school experience, the more likely a child is to finish school, to maintain good self-esteem, and to be successful in later life. Most parents do not know that federal law requires that all public schools test and help children with language or learning disabilities and, if the testing is requested by the school, that it be at no cost to the parents. Even children who are under school age may be covered depending on the programs in your area.

♥ IT IS NORMAL FOR

- preschool-aged children to have high energy levels.
- some children not to listen or do as they are told if they can get away with it.

☞ SEE YOUR PEDIATRICIAN IF

• your child seems impossible to control at home and/or the teacher reports difficulty sitting still, keeping quiet, or finishing assignments.

• you or the teacher think that your child is not achieving his or her potential.

| 7 | SOCIAL DEVELOPMENT |

A. Fear of Strangers, Shyness, Separation Anxiety

Most babies go through a stage somewhere between six months and two years during which they regard strangers—including beloved grandparents—with suspicion if not outright terror. Some children cling tenaciously to their mother's neck or legs, while others run into another room to hide. It may last a few weeks or more than a year.

During this same period, some infants and toddlers become hysterical as soon as Mom is out of sight while others merely need to confirm their mother's nearby presence every once in a while. They may periodically toddle to the doorway of the kitchen for a peek, for example, while playing in the living room.

This is a developmental stage which will disappear in the normal course of events. Indulge your child's need for additional reassurance during this period; if you force your child to be with strangers or to be left alone unnecessarily, you will only make her fears worse. As one of my partners said: there is no need to schedule frustration; it is already built into life.

Spending a few minutes focusing the conversation away from your child will allow time for your child to become more comfortable with a stranger. Have a new babysitter over once or twice to play with your child while you are home before leaving them alone together.

Some older children continue to be overly attached

to a parent or other caregiver and worry and become anxious when they are separated. Such a child may refuse to go to school, worry excessively that harm might befall the parent, or not want to spend the night with a friend away from home. If such fears are persistent and interfere with daily life, it is time to see your pediatrician.

Shyness, on the other hand, is a trait that may very well be present from birth and a permanent part of your child's personality. Recent research suggests that shy children tense up and draw back from new situations and people right after birth, and the pattern continues throughout childhood. Shyness may not be a developmental stage like stranger anxiety, and might not go away. On the other hand, some children may go through a long period of shyness and end up a cheerleader or president of the student body.

If your five-year-old hides behind your leg or prefers to play alone at first when meeting new children, do not make an issue of it. If your child is going through a temporary phase of shyness, let it pass without criticizing the behavior. If it is part of your child's personality, it is important to accept your child as is and allow relationships to develop at their own natural pace. If you wanted an outgoing child but got a shy one, you are the one who should adjust, not your child.

♥ IT IS NORMAL FOR

· children to go through a period of separation anxiety and fear of strangers between six months and two years.

· children to go through periods of shyness and for some children to be shy all through their childhood.

☎ CALL YOUR PEDIATRICIAN IF

· normal stranger anxiety lasts more than a few months.

· your older child is frequently anxious when separated from you.

• your child's shyness is severe enough to prevent normal relationships with other children or seems to restrict his or her life.

B. Lying, Stealing, Setting Fires

When I was about five, I played for hours with my "imaginary brother." I sometimes blamed him for things I was guilty of, but most of the time he just provided companionship to a slightly lonely only child. A part of me knew he was not real, and he disappeared on his own when I was ready to give him up. The tiger in the comic strip "Calvin and Hobbs" which is alive when Calvin is alone but is a stuffed animal when anyone else is around is a perfect example of this.

Imagination is a precious trait. You can still nurture and cherish your child's imagination while you gently point out the difference between real and "pretend."

Under the age of four or five, children have difficulty distinguishing reality from fantasy. That is one of the reasons they may have a persistent fear that interferes with sleep after seeing a cartoon or television show that frightened them. Similarly, they are unclear about what belongs to them and what belongs to others.

Children of this age who take another's toy, who fib or make up stories as though they were real, or who grab something from the store are not on the road to a life of crime. Rather, use the opportunity to teach acceptable attitudes and behavior.

Older children, on the other hand, usually lie for a reason. Fear of punishment for misbehavior may be the only reason, but sometimes it goes deeper than that. Unreasonable expectations from home or school or from the child herself, covering up for a friend or a divorced parent, or subtler reasons may come into play. Often, the child cannot tell you immediately just why it was necessary to lie.

Parents almost always know when their child is lying. My mother used to make me look her in the eye, and that was enough to dispel any illusion that I could fool her. If your older child lies, instead of merely meting out a punishment for lying, tell your child that it is not necessary to lie and try to find out what the trouble really is. If lying is habitual, you may need professional help. The problem is not the lying itself, but rather the *need* to lie. The same thing is true when an older child steals, sets fires, or is destructive.

♥ IT IS NORMAL FOR

- preschoolers to have trouble telling the difference between truth and fantasy, or to try to make things better for themselves by lying.
- older children to occasionally tell a small lie or steal something.

☎ CALL YOUR PEDIATRICIAN IF

- your preschooler's imagination is taking over and interfering with normal relationships with you or with playmates.
- imaginary companions replace real ones.
- your older child habitually lies, steals, or commits destructive acts.

| 8 | MOODINESS AND FEELINGS |

A. "Nobody Likes Me"

The natural, spontaneous parental answer when your child comes home saying, "Nobody likes me," is to point out how incorrect that is: "Why, Jason plays with you all the time. Look how many children came to your birthday party," etc.

Most children are not able to say what is really bothering them, so a child who says "nobody likes me" is usually telling you that this was not a good day for self-esteem. Actually, the child probably feels unlovable, rather than unloved.

At times like these it does not help to point out how incorrect your child's feelings are because feelings are never *wrong*. Provide comfort, reassurance, and commiseration about how awful it is to have those feelings, and let your child know that everyone feels like that at times.

On the other hand, children who really do have problems getting along or who feel rejected by playmates much of the time may have a deeper problem. Sometimes, for example, a child whose parents are divorcing feel that the marriage would have stayed together if only he had not been such a bad child, and he transfers those feelings about himself into his relationships with others.

♥ IT IS NORMAL FOR
- children to feel alone and unlovable sometimes.

☎ CALL YOUR PEDIATRICIAN IF
- this is a frequent or constant problem.

B. Sadness, Frequent Crying, Moodiness, Withdrawal

When Christopher was eight, his mother brought him to my office because he was eating poorly, was irritable, and cried a lot. I asked him to draw a picture of his family, because children can often reveal their feelings better in pictures than in words. Most children this age will draw a brightly shining sun, trees, and grass along with their entire family.

Christopher's picture was done only in black crayon and included a barren rock, rain falling from a cloud, and three people. When I asked him who they were, he said, "My mommy, my daddy, and my brother."

"Where are you?" I asked.

"I don't know," was his heartbreaking answer.

It did not take Sigmund Freud to figure out that Christopher was seriously depressed, probably over his parents' recent divorce. I referred them for counseling, and he is much better now.

Another patient of mine lost his two-year-old brother in a drowning accident when he was five. His parents wanted to spare him all the adult grieving, so they sent him to stay with an aunt until they were over their initial shock and sadness. A year or two later, this child was having crying spells while playing with friends, moping around the house, and acting irritable. The trouble was, he was never able to express his sadness and deal with this terrible loss as his parents did. Once he did that with the help of a child psychologist, he was much better.

Sometimes crying and moodiness have nothing to do with a serious loss such as death or divorce but happen during a period when parents are preoccupied with their own economic problems or job stresses.

The youngest age at which I have recognized serious depression was eighteen months. The child had been cared for during the day by her father, who worked a night shift, while her mother worked the day shift. When the father was transferred to a day shift, a babysitter watched her. This poor toddler sat for hours looking sad, staring into space, and eating little if anything. Once we recognized the reason for her behavior, we had the father leave more gradually to allow her time to adjust, and made sure he spent extra time with her in the evenings.

A subtle illness can also make your child feel bad and look unhappy.

Whatever the reason, depression in children is more common than most people realize. If you suspect that your child is chronically unhappy, see your pediatrician.

♥ IT IS NORMAL FOR
- children to be sad or irritable occasionally.

☎ CALL YOUR PEDIATRICIAN IF
- your child's sadness, inappropriate crying, moodiness, or withdrawal are a frequent, severe, or long-standing problem.

9 | GENITALS AND SEXUAL BEHAVIOR

A. Masturbation

At least one third of all preschool-aged children discover that stimulating their genitals feels good, and will do it to comfort themselves, when they are sleepy or bored, or when watching television. There is nothing abnormal about it, and it is not harmful. By the age of six or so, most children seem to know without being told that this should not be done in public. When a younger child masturbates, your only role should be to emphasize that this is a private activity.

A child who engages in excessive masturbation—that is, one who refuses to confine this behavior to bedroom or bathroom, especially after age five or six, or one who seems disturbed and unhappy along with the onset of this behavior—might be a victim of sexual abuse or some other emotionally upsetting experience. But normal masturbation is not a sign that anything is wrong.

♥ IT IS NORMAL FOR

•   preschool-aged children to masturbate, especially when they are stressed, bored, or tired.

☎ CALL YOUR PEDIATRICIAN IF

•   your child cannot stop masturbating in public, especially over age five or six.

•   your child tries to do the same thing to other children.

•   your child seems unhappy and/or obsessed by masturbation.

•   you suspect that your child was taught to masturbate or seems inordinately fascinated by sexual issues.

B. Interest in Sex

Jason's mother called me with controlled panic in her voice. She had found her five-year-old son in the garage, where he had discovered his father's *Playboy* calendar and was kissing the picture of a voluptuous Miss February.

When she asked him why he was doing that, he answered, "It makes my penis feel good."

"What do you think of that?" she asked me.

"I think you can be reasonably certain that he will be heterosexual," I answered.

Max, the five-year-old son of my good friends, looked at Amy, the twelve-year-old daughter of another friend, and said, "You don't have any breasts." He also told his father that he could kiss Mommy all he wanted but he could not touch her breasts.

Sexuality does not erupt suddenly when puberty begins. Rather, it is a long and gradual process all through childhood. Four- to six-year-olds are particularly overtly although innocently sexual, and it can sometimes shock us.

It is difficult but important to treat childhood sexuality and sexual interest in a matter-of-fact and accepting manner. Explanations can be tricky sometimes, and having a book or two on hand appropriate for your child's age can ease the process if you read them together. Peter Mayles's *Where Did I Come From?*, for example, is one of my favorites.

A pervasive, repetitive, obsessional concern with sex, on the other hand, is cause for concern. Children who have been sexually abused, who witness a sexual act, or who see sexually stimulating material may indirectly let us know by their abnormal concern with sex.

♥ IT IS NORMAL FOR

· children to have an interest in sex, especially beginning around age five.

☎ CALL YOUR PEDIATRICIAN IF

· your child seems abnormally preoccupied with sex.